BY SQUARE & COMPASS

Saga of the Lincoln Home

Wayne C. Temple

Originally entitled:
By Square and Compasses:
The Building of Lincoln's Home and Its Saga

Ashlar Press

By Square & Compass: Saga of the Lincoln Home
1 2 3 4 5 6 7 8 9 10
ISBN: 1878044-80-X
LOC Number: 2001 135464
Mayhaven Publishing
P O Box 557
Mahomet, IL 61853

Printed in Canada

Dedicated To The Memory of

Kathryn and Louis L. Williams
who sponsored the original edition.

See text regarding this photograph of Lincoln on page v and vi, and photo of original Carpentier letter on page 293.

Office of the Secretary of State
Springfield

"This picture of Abraham Lincoln is the one he used during his campaign for the presidency of the United States in 1860. It was taken on a Sunday, June 3, 1860, in the State Capitol building, the structure which is now Sangamon County Courthouse, by Alexander Hesler, a Chicago photographer.

In those days, photographers used wet glass plates and it was common practice for them to reclaim the glass by dipping it in an acid bath to remove the collodion which carried the picture. Somehow, the Lincoln picture escaped that fate.

In 1866, about a year after Lincoln was assassinated, Hesler's studio passed into the hands of George B. Ayers. The full impact of the Emancipator's greatest had not yet dawned on the people, but Ayers decided to keep the negatives as mementos. A year later, he sold the studio and moved to the East, taking the negatives with him. Five weeks later the studio was burned out.

Ayers left the negatives to two daughters, and in 1932, a Philadelphia attorney accepted them in lieu of a fee and a debt of $500 on the estate of one of the daughters. When the attorney attempted to send them by mail to St. Louis, the negatives were broken, making it impossible to obtain any further prints from them. They were turned over to the Smithsonian Institute.

These were believed to be the only extant negatives of the historic picture until the fall of 1952 when King V. Hostick, Springfield collector of historical documents, found a duplicate set of negatives in an assortment of effects he bought in Philadelphia at the estate of Ayers. This print was made from one of those negatives."

Charles F. Carpentier, Secretary of State

Table of Contents

"Tool Box" (c. 1891) made of Walnut lumber taken from the original cornice of the Lincoln Home. It is owned by Lynda Selde of New York City. Photo by Matt Wood. Copyrighted by Luann Elvey.

Preface

For over twenty years, I searched to find conclusive evidence showing that Page Eaton actually helped to construct the house later purchased by the Lincolns in Springfield, Illinois. My efforts were at last been rewarded with success. In the process, I discovered other workmen who labored in the Lincoln home from time to time. To these names I have added those who once lived in the home.

As my late father, Howard Milton Temple, often said, "Even a blind hog finds acorns if he roots!" And I, indeed, rooted through many a woods filled with primary sources. When the elusive facts at last came to light, it turned out that Page Eaton had worked as the junior partner on this construction project which was actually bossed by his father, John Eaton, Jr, corroborating my earlier findings.

During the many years of tedious labor, numerous helpful persons aided me with this task of scholarship. No successful writer accomplishes much by his own efforts alone.

The late James Nelson Adams, of the Illinois State

Historical Library, originally discovered one of the newspaper stories concerning Page Eaton as a carpenter and unselfishly presented it to the present author.

Mr. & Mrs. Charles W. Hodge put him in contact with a descendant, Ruth Weitzel Ellis, who has Page Eaton's manuscript account of his travels and labors.

The author's beautiful wife, Sunderine (Wilson) Temple, first talked to Mr. & Mrs. Marshall Dillon Brooke of Palatine, Illinois. Mr. Brooke, a registered pharmacist, is a great grandson of Page Eaton and has a valuable collection of family manuscripts and photographs.

Thomas Matchan Brooke of Orlando, Florida, completed a volume entitled *George and Maria Brooke*. It deals with the Civil War career of Capt. George Darrah Brooke, Sr., and is most helpful to researchers since it reproduces many of the original documents. He has also compiled another book called *George Darrah Brooke, Jr., 1853-1922*. It is filled with the papers of this famous man.

James L. Hansen, at the State Historical Society of Wisconsin, helped track down descendants of Knud Olsen, supplied census data, and verified an unidentified newspaper clipping. He also helped with Dr. G. Wendlandt.

Bernice M. Bordeaux first put the author on the trail of Olsen and furnished various photos and family research.

Edna McMahan Secrest, Michael "Mick" Bernasek, and Manker Harris aided the author in obtaining the correct date of death for Henry Dresser.

Milton D. Dirst has always gladly opened various Masonic records to the author.

Dr. Lloyd Ostendorf of Dayton, Ohio, the world's greatest illustrator of Lincoln, provided special art work for this monograph. One of his most recent portraits of Lincoln is in the Museum of Our National Heritage, Lexington, Massachusetts.

Ruth L. Hutchcraft skillfully typed and retyped the manuscript from spoiled pages that had been polished and corrected numerous times between the lines.

Louis L. Williams encouraged the author to transform this manuscript into a small book when the latter spoke to the Philalethes Society at Bob Johnson's Restaurant in Bloomington, Illinois, on February 7, 1983. His topic to the Society was "How To Write a Book."

At the invitation of Dean Donald R. Eldred and Professor James E. Davis, the author used this dissertation for his Convocation Lecture in Crispin Hall at Illinois College in Jacksonville on the evening of February 17, 1983. (This was his second appearance on campus as a Convocation speaker.) He was honored by a lecture room filled with professors, administrators, students, and townsfolk. Prominent in this audience were his Brothers of Phi Alpha Fraternity. Back on January 26, 1859, this ancient "Literary Society" made Abraham Lincoln a member, and on May 22, 1982, it presented the author with membership in recognition of his writings and lectures on the Sixteenth President. He is extremely proud to be a fraternity brother of his hero, A. Lincoln.

Since John Eaton, Jr., was a veteran of the War of 1812, Commander and Doctor Wilbur T. Reece of Post 32 asked the author to lecture to his local American Legion Post concerning this topic. He did so on Friday evening, February 4, 1983, to help the Post observe "Americanism Month."

Many hours of research have taken place in the Illinois State Archives, the Illinois State Historical Library, and Lincoln Library. All staffs have been most helpful.

Winfred "Doc" Helm, David O. Haaker, and Al Von Behren have reproduced photographs. So has Harry (Bud) Roberts taken a photo for this book.

Prof. Raymond H. Hammes has shared his insights with me on this project. For this intellectual coöperation, the author is grateful.

Archie Motley, Curator of Manuscripts at the Chicago Historical Society, assisted with the Tiltons in Chicago.

Maynard Upton drew designs for the covers and title pages.

Leland Hilligoss, History and Genealogy Department of the St. Louis Public Library, answered several questions most quickly and effectively.

Mary Ann Lamm, Recorder of Deeds for Sangamon County, freely opened the records under her custody to the author.

Robert V. Hillman shared his research on Ludlum with the author.

Bradley S. Eckols read census material in the Illinois State Archives.

Thanks to Dolores M. Johnson and Col. Robert Graham for access to the records of Oak Ridge Cemetery.

Greg Schou located the funeral records for Jacob D. Akard; Greg works at Boardman-Smith, South Grand at Glenwood, Springfield, Ill.

Clair E. and Harriette C. Wyman researched the Tiltons in Keene, New Hampshire, and took photographs of the railroad bridge built by Lucian Tilton and the gravestones in the cemetery at Keene.

Stanley T. Kusper, Jr., Cook County Clerk, gave scholarly assistance to the author. Thanks also to Michael Fish of his office.

Lisa T. McKuin, Student Records Auditor, Washington University in St. Louis, Mo., searched files.

Dr. Paul G. Anderson, Archivist, Washington University School of Medicine, St. Louis, Mo., located the student records of Dr. Wendlandt.

Judith P. Reid, The Library of Congress, traced Oldroyd in Washington, D.C.

Edward J. Russo, Sangamon Valley Collection, Lincoln Library at Springfield, Illinois, was most helpful; Karen Graff also helped.

Grace E. Baker, Librarian at The Society of California Pioneers, San Francisco, discovered the exact death date for Ludlum.

Kenneth Shanks, Archivist at the Federal Archives & Records Center in Chicago, uncovered the Oldroyd bankruptcy case.

Robert A. Klinger, Grand Secretary of the Grand Lodge, F. & A. M., of California, checked the published proceedings for C. Ludlum. The earthquake and fire in 1906 had destroyed the original manuscripts.

Judy Sheldon, Reference Librarian, California Historical Society, San Francisco, answered numerous questions with expertise.

Lyle H. Paisley, Grand Secretary of the Grand Lodge, A. F. & M., of Illinois allowed the author to have free access to the manuscripts and published proceedings.

Prof. George H. Miller of Ripon College dug out the facts on Mason Brayman in that part of the country.

Betty Fox at the Carnegie-Stout Public Library in Dubuque, Iowa, searched valiantly for clues to the Hannons.

Robert B. Brandl, Register of Deeds in Manitowoc, Wisconsin, supplied the marriage record for Dr. Wendlandt.

La Verne Marshall searched the city cemetery of Princeton, Wisconsin, until she found the stone for Dr. Wendlandt and his second wife.

Dorothy H. Tucker and William I. Richter located the burial place of Hedwig (Richter) Wendlandt in Evergreen Cemetery, Manitowoc, Wisconsin.

Jean Skinner, C.G.R.S., found numerous Wisconsin records for this study.

Col. Noel R. Barton, The Genealogical Society of Utah, supplied the 1850 census of Ohio.

In many books, the authors ignore vital parts of their subjects' lives. Too often these writers purposely refuse to identify the religion, political party or fraternal memberships of their heroes. And yet these very controversial elements of life actually shape the pattern of behavior for every human being. To truly know a person, one must first examine his organizations and his friends. Armed with this knowledge, we can better understand why a man or woman acted as he or she did under certain circumstances. For instance, Masonry is a way of life, and so readers will find fraternal identifications in the body of this book as well as in the lengthy footnotes. Also, this author has in every case attempted to learn the religious and political preference for every major figure mentioned in this work. Such a task has not been easy, but it is felt that the results are well worth the effort which has been expended to dig out this elusive information.

The title for this treatise comes from the fact that the square and compasses were the most important measuring tools used in constructing or remodeling the Lincoln home. Then, too, so many of the builders, occupants or persons involved with this residence were either speculative or operative masons that it was thought this title fit the story extremely well.

Readers will discover that this volume is written from many previously unknown sources and is a new contribution to the Lincoln saga. It is hoped that they will enjoy this tale as much as the author did in assembling it, writing it down, and lecturing about it.

The preceding was written on February 12, 1984, at the 175th Anniversary of Abraham Lincoln's birth.

Since this volume first appeared in 1984, the original edition has long been out of print. Due to popular demand, it has been published again with additional information on the Lincoln Home at Springfield.

This book is the only full-length study of the building and occupancy of the only residence ever owned by Abraham and Mary Lincoln. Both the State of Illinois and the Federal Government have lovingly restored this vintage structure, and now the National Park Service welcomes thousands and thousands of visitors each year by escorting them through the Lincolns' house. It is one of the most important Lincoln shrines in the United States.

Through the efforts of Doris Replogle Wenzel of Mayhaven Publishing, this revised edition of this historical saga has been reissued for the use of tourists and scholars who study the Lincolns and their times.

Wayne C. Temple, Springfield, Illinois, July, 2001

PORTION OF E. ILES ADDITION
TO SPRINGFIELD

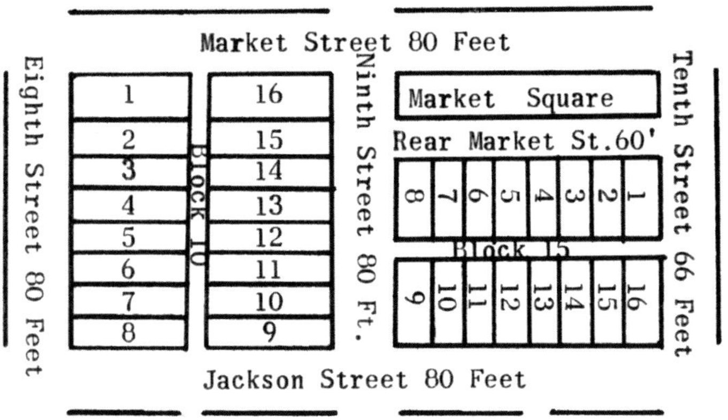

This plat shows a portion of the E. Iles Addition to Springfield surveyed by John B. Watson in 1836. The Rev. Mr. Charles Dresser purchased Lot No. 8 of Block 10 in 1839 and then later acquired ten feet off the south side of Lot No. 7. Abraham Lincoln purchased this real estate and house in 1844.

Rev. & Mrs. Charles Dresser posed for a Daguerreotype artist sometime after they sold their residence to the Lincolns.This fine photograph is in the Conry Collection of the Illinois State Historical Library. Copy by Al Von Behren.

Reverend Dresser Builds a Residence

Abraham and Mary Lincoln's historic Quaker-brown-colored frame home in Springfield, Illinois, lies in Block Ten of the Elijah Iles Addition to the original town. But they were not the builders or first owners of this famous dwelling. It has an even longer past.

By the eleventh day of April in 1836, John B. Watson, Deputy Surveyor for Sangamon County, had completed his mapping of this new section. Elijah Iles, the prosperous proprietor, then signed the finished plat before Thomas Moffett, a Justice of the Peace, on April 21, and the Recorder of Deeds accepted it and filed the same on June 22 that year. Market (now called Capitol), Eighth, Ninth and Jackson streets bounded Block Ten. Watson laid off all these thoroughfares eighty feet in width with a sixteen-foot alley running from north to south down the middle of the block, and each had a forty-foot frontage with a depth of 152 feet.[1]

In April of 1838, the Reverend Mister Charles Dresser (1800-1865), his wife, Louisa (Walker) Withers, and their

Henry Dresser (1813-1898), a younger brother of Charles Dresser, labored as a carpenter and builder. He may have talked with Charles about his proposed residence, but Henry did not build it. Rarely in those days did an "architect" construct a private dwelling in Springfield. From the Conry Collection in the Illinois State Historical Library. Copy by Al Von Behren.

two sons, David Walker and Thomas Withers, arrived safely in Springfield from Halifax Court House, Virginia. He came to the new capital city to preside over the Protestant Episcopal Church as Rector. Born February 24, 1800, in Pomfret, Connecticut, the son of Nathan and Rebecca (Leffingwell) Dresser, he had graduated from prestigious Brown University in 1823 and had been ordained in 1829 after studying theology in Virginia with Bishop William Meade (1789-1862).[2]

With a growing family, the Rev. Dresser needed a substantial home to show off his new position as a leader of the town. Therefore, on April 23, 1839, for $300, he purchased Lot 8 in Block 10 of the E. Iles Addition from Dr. Gershom Jayne (1791-1867) and his wife, Sybil.[3] Dr. Jayne, no doubt, had bought this particular lot for speculation since no structure had previously been erected there when Dresser and his consort acquired it. Coming to Springfield in 1820, Dr. Jayne practiced medicine widely as the first physician in this whole area. Indeed, from July 20 until August 27, 1827, he served as the Surgeon of the Fever River Expedition. (Later, that river became known as the Galena.) This brave volunteer force of mounted riflemen fought under the command of Col. Thomas M. Neale against the wily Indians in northwestern Illinois.

Because the Rev. Mr. Dresser had a younger brother, Henry (1813-1898), who sold his services as an architect, several authors quite naturally have speculated—or even assumed—that he actually planned or built the house constructed for Rev. Dresser on the northeast corner of Eighth and Jackson streets. Although Henry did come to Springfield in 1838—the same year as his brother—he never once, to our knowledge, boasted of having put up the residence where the Lincolns later lived. He had an excellent opportunity to do so when his autobiographical sketch came out in the *Portrait and Biographical Album of Morgan and Scott Counties, Ills.* (Chicago: Chapman Brothers, 1889) on pages 534 and 535. Henry Dresser did relate that he had erected "the highest [Henry] Clay [political campaign] pole in the State at Springfield, and which reared its top to the height of 226 feet from the ground." That engineering feat certainly would have seemed pallid to Henry Dresser if he really had some connection with the home that A. Lincoln lived in at Springfield. (Charles Dresser's life story exulted greatly over the fact that "he solemnized the marriage of Abraham Lincoln and Mary Todd, Nov. 4, 1842.") The Dressers were not above some well-earned bragging.

Those writers who have assumed Henry Dresser drew house plans for his brother have no proof whatsoever to substantiate such a seemingly-logical theory. Almost any competent carpenter, brick mason or stonemason in those years of long apprenticeships could construct a simple dwelling without formal plans, or close supervision, of a professional architect. In that lusty period of time, most full-time architects paused only briefly in the smaller towns of the Midwest or else they turned their hands to other vocations. Few contracts for building ever came to them. During the finishing of the State House at Springfield in 1845, Henry Dresser gave his expert advice as a "skillful workman."

As further corroboration of this conclusion, when Henry Dresser joined the Freemasons of Springfield Lodge Number Four in 1846, he gave his occupation as that of a carpenter. (He took a demit December 21, 1851, and later transferred his membership to Naples, Illinois. When the Charter of Naples Lodge No. 68 was arrested on September 16, 1892, Henry was a Deacon.) And after he left Springfield in 1848, he labored as a farmer, director and supplier of building materials for a railroad, drainer of farm lands, steamboat captain, carpenter, stonemason, bridge builder, member of the Illinois General Assembly, county judge and politician. He did manage to become the superintendent for the construction of the Deaf and Dumb Asylum at Jacksonville, a rare return to his profession as an architect. Probate records in Scott County show that he died at Bluffs on July 21, 1898.

For another example, John Francis Rague (1799-1877) turned up at Springfield, Illinois, in 1831. He hailed from New York City[4] where he had trained as an architect. But without a demand for his building skills, Rague eventually opened a bakery and accepted mundane town-government positions in order to support himself and his family. His only

Sarah M. Eaton, (Mrs. Joseph Patterson), sister of Page Eaton and John Bainbridge Eaton. Photo courtesy of Marshall D. Brooke

known major building project in those early years at Springfield turned out to be the State House contract which political and church friends helped him obtain from the commissioners. Its cornerstone went into place on 4 July, 1837.

Now—for the very first time—it can be proved conclusively from a primary manuscript source that John Eaton, Jr. (1791-1846), and his son, Page Eaton (1821-1899), put up the now-famous frame dwelling which the Lincolns later purchased. The history of this New England family goes back to the *Mayflower* and can be traced through the laborious scratchings of Page Eaton's own ink pen. These informative writings, now owned by Ruth Weitzel Ellis of Sarasota, Florida, reveal that John Eaton, Jr., established a carriage factory and a carpenter's shop in his hometown of Bradford, Merrimack County, New Hampshire. After serving his country in the War of 1812 as a Private in Danforth's 45th Infantry, John returned home proudly, got married to Mary Cook, and continued his crafts until the family plant burned about the year 1815. As a result of these misfortunes, the Eatons eventually moved on to Concord where John erected another carriage factory and carpenter's shop. Page Eaton was born October 25, 1821. Then the family shop again fell to fire in 1825 but soon rose again. However, it, too, went up in smoke during the year 1837.

Father and son then decided to abandon New Hampshire and make their headquarters in Illinois where their luck would certainly be better. They started their long journey west on February 25, 1838, while the crunchy white snow lay three feet deep upon the frozen ground. They sledded into Buffalo, New York, on March 15 and secured employment with Benjamin Cook, uncle to Page Eaton on his Mother's side of the clan. Cook, a builder with a large clientele, gave them work for two months. At the end of that period, John traded his sleigh for a buggy and set off by road to Illinois, while Page remained in Buffalo, laboring alone as a carpenter, until November. In that month of Thanksgiving he boarded a ship and sailed through the lakes to Chicago. From this inland port city he walked overland to where his Father then resided: Paris, Edgar County, Illinois. Page later remarked that since no railroads existed then, he trudged the weary 168 miles on foot to rejoin his Dad.

Their carpentry jobs finished there, John and Page Eaton traveled westward to Springfield in May of 1839 and commenced to construct a residence on Eighth Street for the Episcopal minister. Their employer was, of course, none other than Charles Dresser whom Eaton correctly identified as having come to Springfield the previous year.

As can happen so easily without a prior survey, the builders and the Rev. Dresser ultimately discovered to their great chagrin that by facing the front of the house toward Eighth Street, where the lot extended only 40 feet in width, they either did not have enough room to follow the building plans or else they had already crossed the invisible property line to the north with their foundations. To remedy this embarrassing situation as quickly as possible, on August 21, 1839, Dresser paid Francis and Emeline M. Webster, Jr., $90 for a fraction of their Lot No. 7, being a "Strip ten feet wide off of the South side (running from East to West) of said Lot."[5] In those days of respect for a churchman, who would have refused an ardent plea from a man-of-the-cloth that found himself in such a difficult situation? Nevertheless, the preacher paid a slight premium for this ten feet of land. If it had been prorated exactly, the price would have amounted to only $75. Yet, naturally, the Webster's lot had been diminished and had become much less valuable to a future buyer. Previous writers upon this subject have assumed that Dresser started building in the fall of the year after his second purchase of real estate. However, Page Eaton reported the building as having been commenced in May. What sensible builder in those years of slower production would have waited until late August to start construction on a house?

In June of 1974, John L. Raynolds, Jr., of Raynolds & Walschleger at 1625 South Sixth Street in Springfield, Illinois, a registered land surveyor, resurveyed Block 10 for the National Park Service which now owns the Lincoln Home National Historic Site. He discovered that the Lincoln dwelling extended 6.15 feet beyond the northern boundary of Lot Eight.

Perhaps the construction of his home cost Dresser more than he had estimated, or else he had previously invested his ready cash in other real estate. Anyhow, on July 22, 1840, he borrowed $900 from Ebenezer H. Sawyer of Windham County, Connecticut, and gave the lender a promissory note which carried the vigorous interest of twelve per cent. Dresser's borrowed money may have gone to the Eaton's for their labors on the house.

By July 7th of the following year, the Rev. Dresser determined to liquidate his debt which needed to be repaid by the 22nd of that month. He therefore offered his house for sale "on accommodating terms" and further announced that if it did not sell prior to the first day of September, it would then be for rent.[6] When neither a buyer nor a renter answered his pleading advertisement, the indebted minister by necessity remained in his recently-completed residence.

Later, on February 15, 1843, Sawyer forced Dresser to execute a formal mortgage to protect his $900 loan. As security, the Episcopal Minister put up the East Half of the Southeast Quarter of Section 27, the East Half of the West Half of the Northeast Quarter of Section 34, and the West Half of the Southeast Quarter of Section 34, all in Township Fifteen North, Range Four West of the Third Principal Meridian—farm land lying southeast of Springfield in Rochester Township of Sangamon County. In addition to these 200 acres of real estate, he offered as collateral his prized home at Eighth and Jackson streets: Lot 8 and a quarter of Lot 7 in Block 10.[7]

References

1 E. Iles Addition to Springfield, Plat, Recorder of Deeds, Sangamon County Bldg.

2 John Carroll Power, ed., *History of the Early Settlers of Sangamon County, Illinois* (Springfield: Edwin A. Wilson & Co., 1876), 268-269.

3 Deed Record, O, 284, Recorder of Deeds, Sangamon Co. Bldg.

4 Eliza M. Rague vs. John F. Rague, March Term, 1853, Sangamon Co. Circuit Court Records, MSS., IRAD, University of Illinois at Springfield Library.

5 Deed Record, O, 585-586.

6 *Sangamo Journal* (Springfield), July 9, 1841, p. 3, c. 2.

7 Deed Record, U, 109-110.

Capitol Complex
Central City of Springfield

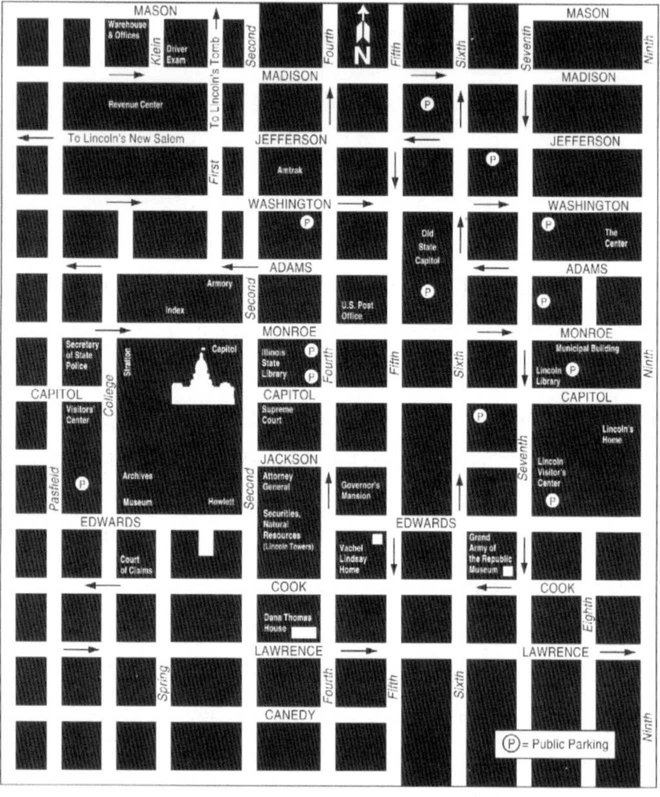

Several streets have been closed since Lincoln's day. Third Street is narrow with a railroad running down the middle of it. Eighth and Jackson have been closed at the Lincoln home, but pedestrians may still use them. Likewise, Adams is closed to the South of the Old State Capitol, forming a mall. The top of this map is North. From a drawing prepared for Jim Edgar, Secretary of State [Later Governor of Illinois].

The Lincolns Buy a Home

When Lawyer Lincoln and Mary Todd patched up their broken romance and decided to get married, they asked the Rev. Mr. Dresser to perform the ceremony at the so-called mansion of Mr. and Mrs. Ninian Wirt Edwards (Mary's sister, Elizabeth Porter (Todd) Edwards, and brother-in-law) on November 4, 1842. While making the vital arrangements for the Minister's services, Lincoln certainly paid a call upon Dresser in his domicile on Eighth Street. Although this very residence remained up for sale, Mary's betrothed did not have nearly enough cash to acquire it for her. No, instead of purchasing a home, the newlyweds took up their humble housekeeping at the Globe Tavern.[8]

Gradually, by thrift and gift, the Lincolns built up some savings after the husband's old New Salem debts had finally been liquidated. Once more they seriously and earnestly examined the Dresser property and decided this time that they could afford it. On January 16, 1844, Barrister Lincoln contracted with Charles Dresser to buy this home and receive possession by April 1 that year. The Lincolns agreed to pay Dresser $1,200 plus a lot west of the Public Square owned jointly by Lincoln and Stephen Trigg Logan, his law partner.[9]

Ninian W. and Elizabeth P. Edwards had sold this particular town lot to Logan & Lincoln for $400 on March 16, 1842—its legal description being the East Half of the West Half of Lot Number Six in Block Fourteen of the City of Springfield.[10] On it sat a building which Hamilton A. Hough (pronounced "Huff,"[11]) utilized as a shop for his carpentry business. (Hough had attempted to construct the main stairs for the State House, and he was a member of The Springfield Mechanic's Union.) Both contracting parties agreed that "Said Dresser takes upon himself to arrange with said Hough for the possession of said shop and premises."[12]

As earnest money, Lincoln handed Dresser $750 on February 5, 1844. The latter signed a receipt showing that he had received the cash and that if he failed to deliver the property to Lincoln on time, the money would be refunded plus twelve per cent interest. S.M. Tinsley cosigned the receipt and bound himself to see that the contract was fulfilled. (Seth Tinsley operated a store and owned the building where Logan & Lincoln kept their law office.) Shortly after this transaction, Lincoln informed his father-in-law, Robert Smith Todd in Lexington, Kentucky, "that he was going to housekeeping." Todd expressed himself as being most pleased with this venture. From the tenor of a letter written by Todd at this time, it is easy to see that he held great fondness for the tall lawyer who had married his daughter Mary.[13]

This drawing, by Xavier C. Meyer of the Illinois Division of Parks & Memorials of the Lincoln Home, is taken from the *Journal of the Illinois State Historical* Society, XLVIII, 14.

April 1 in 1844 came and went without the contract for purchase being fully executed. Twenty-two days later, however, on April 23, Abraham and Mary Lincoln plus Stephen T. and America Logan met and conveyed the lot in question to Dresser for $300 credit on the home.[14] That figure represented a depreciation of $100 since Logan & Lincoln had acquired the tract back in March of 1842.

In some unknown manner—probably by cash—the Lincolns paid off the remaining price of the house. Charles and Louisa W. Dresser then presented them the deed on May 2, 1844. In total, their home cost the Lincolns $1,500.[15]

Lincoln, an exacting and knowledgeable lawyer, stated in his contract for deed that Dresser should convey "by a clear title in fee simple, the entire premises (ground and improvements) in Springfield, on which said Dresser now resides." And the buyer must have personally examined the deed record at the office of the Recorder of Deeds in the Courthouse. But that legal document did not have the mortgage recorded in the margin of the book, as was the usual practice. While the original deed occupied pages in Volume O, the mortgage had been recorded separately in Volume U. Either by inquiry or rumor, Lincoln learned of this lien upon his newly-acquired property. No doubt he immediately insisted that Dresser clear the title without fail. Since the Minister had cash in his possession from the sale of his house to Lincoln, he could do this transaction easily. Or perhaps he had forwarded the debt money plus interest to Windham County, Connecticut, and the mortgage holder had been remiss in handling the removal procedure in faraway Springfield, Illinois.

Upon being prodded by Dresser, Ebenezer H. Sawyer executed a power of attorney in favor of Robert Irwin of Sangamon County. Irwin, a dry-goods merchant with John

Williams, in turn, cleared the title of its mortgage on 17 August 1844. He had this vital instrument duly recorded in Springfield on the thirtieth of that same month.[16] At long last, the young Lincolns owned an impressive home free of debt and located in a most respectable neighborhood. It stood one and a half storeys tall, with sleeping rooms in the half story.

At least once, Abraham Lincoln dramatically referred to his house and lot in a most prominent and public way. While criticizing the Democratic President, James K. Polk, for his inexact legal description of the Texas border with Mexico, the Honorable A. Lincoln made reference to what was most certainly his own property back in Springfield. Standing at his full height in the august House of Representatives Chamber in Washington, D.C., the witty Lincoln exclaimed to his colleagues on January 12, 1848: "I know a man, not very unlike myself, who exercises jurisdiction over a piece of land between the Wabash and the Mississippi; and yet so far is this from being all there is between those rivers, that it is just one hundred and fifty-two feet long by fifty wide, and no part of it much within a hundred miles of either. He has a neighbor between him and the Mississippi—that is, just across the street, in that direction—whom, I am sure, he could neither persuade nor force to give up his habitation; but which nevertheless, he could certainly annex, if it were to be done, by merely standing on his own side of the street and claiming it, or even, sitting down, and writing a deed for it."

Without much doubt, Lincoln used his own real estate as his example. Its legal description matches his own exactly, even to the fifty feet in width. Other lots would have merely contained the standard forty feet in frontage on Eighth Street.

This original house of native hardwood would come to hold many sacred memories for the tall Lincoln and his short wife. Except for Robert T., all their children would be born here: Edward Baker Lincoln, March 10, 1846; William Wallace Lincoln, December 21, 1850; and Thomas Lincoln, April 4, 1853. Robert Todd Lincoln had been born in the Globe Tavern on August 1, 1843.

References

8 Roy P. Basler, Marion D. Pratt and Lloyd A. Dunlap, eds., *The Collected Works of Abraham Lincoln* (New Brunswick: Rutgers Univ. Press, 1953), I, 325.

9 Facsimile of contract in Harry E. Pratt, *The Personal Finances of Abraham Lincoln* (Springfield: Abraham Lincoln Assoc., 1943), 64. The printed text on page 63 has an incorrect date of "January 7."

10 Deed Record, S, 502-503. Pratt and previous writers copying from him have misdated the deed as "March 17." See page 63.

11 The U.S. Census of 1840, for Springfield, Sangamon Co., Ill., p. 9, l. 25, spelled his name as he pronounced it: "Huff." A carpenter, he was between 20 and 30 years of age in that census year. He has been misidentified as "Henry A. Hough," but Lincoln clearly wrote "Hamilton A. Hough" in the Deed Record, V, 301-302. The census corroborates a Hamilton Hough in Springfield and Hamilton A. Hough contracted, August 24, 1840, to build stairs in the State House. Although he was paid in part, his stairs had to be redone. MS., State House File, Illinois State Archives. (Hough was a Freemason— a member of Springfield Lodge No. 4.)

12 Facsimile of document in Pratt, *Personal Finances*, 64. Sotheby Parke Bernet, Inc., of New York sold this contract at auction on November 28, 1979. A facsimile is shown on page 144 of their catalogue for The Roy P. Crocker Collection. Minute Book, The Springfield Mechanic's Union, 193, MS., Illinois State Historical Library.

13 Pratt, *Personal Finances*, 65; R.S. Todd to Ninian W. Edwards, Lexington, Ky., Mar. 13, 1844, MS., Robert Todd Lincoln Coll., Ill. State Hist. Lib.

14 Deed Record, V, 301-302.

15 *Ibid.*, V, 300-301.

16 *Ibid.*, V, 496-497. Dresser went to live on Seventh, between Jefferson and Monroe.

Page Eaton as drawn by Dr. Lloyd Ostendorf from photographs of various family members. No photograph of Page Eaton has been found. However, one of his sister, Sarah, exists in the collection of Marshall D. Brooke. From this photo and ones of Page Eaton's daughter, the artist has composed a probable likeness of the young man who helped construct the house later purchased by Abraham Lincoln.

Page Eaton and His Descendants

The Eatons decided to establish their business permanently in Illinois. So, in the fall of 1840, John returned to the East for the rest of his family. They settled down in Petersburg, some twenty-two miles northwest of Springfield, where John, and his sons Page and Hiram G. (1814-ca. 1860), put up the new Courthouse and a church. (Menard County had been set off from Sangamon on February 15, 1839, and needed an official building in which to conduct the county's business.)

With their profits, the Eatons purchased eighty acres of land west of Petersburg and farmed for part of their living. But in the fall of 1844, Page Eaton moved over to Beardstown (Cass County) on the Illinois River and established a shop there. In that town he helped build the Courthouse where Lincoln later cleared William "Duff" Armstrong of a murder charge. On November 16, 1857, the famous case of the People v. William Armstrong opened in the Cass County Circuit Court at Beardstown on a change

Margaret Ann (Lee) Eaton, wife of Page Eaton, in later years. From the collection of Marshall D. Brooke.

of venue from Mason County. "Duff" Armstrong was the son of Lincoln's old New Salem friends, John "Jack" and Hannah Armstrong. In the Black Hawk War, "Jack" Armstrong had served as one of Capt. A. Lincoln's sergeants. Counselor Lincoln finally cleared "Duff" of the murder charge on May 7, 1858, by using an almanac to discredit the prosecution's star witness. (This famous structure still stands, although the county seat is now at Virginia.)

After the year 1846, Page Eaton conducted and managed his own business; his Father had died while erecting a mill at Naples, Illinois, in that year. His Mother died in 1853.[17] Although Springfield served as the hub of his construction activities, Page Eaton resided at Beardstown at the time of his marriage to Margaret Ann Lee of Springfield on May 25, 1852.[18] When his second shop burned in 1853, he went back to Springfield. Later, he reported himself as operating a carpenter's and joiner's shop on Monroe Street, opposite Manning's Carriage Factory in Springfield. He boasted of being "prepared to raise buildings without injuring the plastering."[19] After that, he advertised for additional carpenters, because he had the contract as "architect and builder" of the new brick German Methodist Church at the southeast corner of Seventh and Mason.[20]

Three years following the Civil War, Page Eaton gave a press interview to a reporter from the *Utica* (Illinois) *Herald* concerning the building of the home later owned by Abraham and Mary Lincoln. His reminiscences—solicited for the third anniversary of Lincoln's assassination—found their way into the columns of the Belvidere (Illinois) *Standard* for April 14, 1868, page one, where they have survived to this day. "I am a carpenter," related Eaton, "and built [Lincoln's] house for him." With those words, the interview continued with much interesting information.

When this author first published Eaton's newspaper remarks as a booklet,[21] Lincoln scholars promptly ignored the new information and reasoned that this chap had been much too young to have labored as a carpenter on the Dresser dwelling, constructed originally as a story-and-a-half structure. True, Page Eaton had been born on the twenty-fifth day of October in 1821 and would have been only seventeen-plus when the home started to rise. Nevertheless, it must be remembered that in those palmy frontier days, mere youths often assumed the heavy responsibilities of serious and responsible adults. As we now know, Page Eaton had indeed worked by himself in Buffalo prior to his removal to Illinois.

In all probability, Page Eaton certainly never intended the inquiring journalist to indicate to the public that he had acted alone in the construction. Page mentioned his Father when writing out his own history of the events. The reporter, no doubt, edited these remarks out of the story. No, he hammered and sawed as the junior carpenter on the job, as he himself stated in writing. However, the basic parts of Eaton's printed interview stand as a primary source of Lincolniana.

Upon the death of Page Eaton in Springfield at his residence (909 South Fifth Street) on December 19, 1899, at 9:20 p.m., his lengthy obituary reiterated the historical information that he had constructed the house where Abraham Lincoln had resided with his beloved family. "One of the old buildings of Springfield which Mr. Eaton erected," declared the editor with authority, "is no other than the Lincoln homestead, which building has an interesting history, having been the abode of Lincoln. Springfield has always been proud of this homestead."[22]

Cause of death was termed as "old age." Eaton had passed his seventy-eighth birthday in October. The Reverend D.F. Howe of the First Methodist Episcopal Church conducted the funeral services three days later with burial being made in Oak Ridge Cemetery. Surviving—in addition to his widow—were four children: Grace D. (Mrs. A.K. Stacy) of Springfield; William C. Eaton of Chicago; Kate D. (Mrs. Walter E. Powell) of Chicago; and Lelia Anna (Mrs. George D. Brooke) of St. Paul.[23]

Since that time in 1868 when Page Eaton first revealed to a reporter that he had built the Lincoln home, thirty-one years had passed before his obituary repeated this fundamental fact. But in all that time—as far as can be ascertained—not one single individual ever stepped forward to deny Eaton's claim or even alter the record in the slightest detail. Reminiscences given out long years after Abraham Lincoln's death tend to be suspect until corroborating information can be amassed as support. In this case, even

Dresser's widow resided in Springfield in 1868. She definitely knew the contractor of her old home at Eighth and Jackson. Then, too, Mrs. Abraham Lincoln still sojourned in Chicago and would have known the truth of the matter.

Because there have been no contemporary gainsayers to Eaton's statements, his testimony still stands undisputed and undenied. Certainly his explanation clears up one more mystery in the unending interest in Lincoln's fascinating life.

Margaret Ann Eaton, the widow of Page Eaton, lived on until 11:30 p.m. on April 21, 1901. She passed away in the home of her daughter and son-in-law, A.K. Stacy, at 939 South Fifth Street in Springfield. "Old age" caused her demise, reported a local newspaper. Being a member of the First Methodist Episcopal Church, the minister of that congregation conducted the burial services, and her body was interred at Oak Ridge Cemetery beside that of her husband.[24]

A daughter of Thomas E. Lee, Margaret Ann had been born August 12, 1829, on a farm near Milford, Delaware. She came to Springfield, Illinois, with her father and family at the age of 9. From an examination of the census, it would appear that her mother had died before 1850. At that time, her father kept a livery stable and thereby supported his son, James, and the two daughters, Margaret A. and Lydia.[25]

One daughter of Margaret and Page Eaton led a history-making life. The older one, Lelia Anna, born in Beardstown, Illinois—an important port upon the Illinois River—on February 12, 1853, married George Darrah Brooke, Jr. He was the son of George D. and Maria (Lutz) Brooke, Sr., and had been born in Philadelphia on November 5, 1853. In that "City of Brotherly Love," the father labored as a carpenter. But two years after the birth of George, Jr., the family trekked westward to Baldwin City in eastern Kansas. When the Civil War came, the Brooke family reside in Lawrence. George, Sr., promptly won election as the First Lieutenant of Company A in the Third Regiment of Kansas Volunteers. Because of a consolidation order, the Third went into the Tenth Regiment. On September 28, 1862, Brooke received promotion to Captain and commanded Company C. At that time, the Regiment was fighting Indians in the West. However, in May of 1864, the Tenth went to St. Louis as Provost Guard for that city. Captain Brooke commanded the Myrtle Street Prison. Later, he returned to the field and fought Confederates. After much action, Brooke was mustered out of service on June 16, 1865, at Montgomery, Alabama.

In 1864, Capt. Brooke had moved his family to St. Louis, Missouri. There, George, Jr., went to high school and entered the Polytechnic Division of Washington University. He majored in civil engineering and graduated in 1875. For the degree of Civil Engineer, Brooke submitted a thesis on June 13th that year. It ran to fifty-four pages and was entitled "Low Service Pumping Engine, No. 3, Recently constructed at the Fulton Foundry, by Gerard B. Allen, & Co., for the Board of Commissioners of the St. Louis Water Works."

The family of George Darrah Brooke, Jr. Front row, left to right: George Darrah Brooke, Jr., William Stacy Brooke, and Lelia Anna (Eaton) Brooke. Rear row, left to right: Charles Walter Brooke, Sr. and Katherine Estelle Brooke. Photo from collection of Marshall D. Brooke.

Following graduation, Brooke found employment on various surveying and engineering jobs, including work at the mouth of the Mississippi River and at the marshes of the Red River. But in June of 1876, he accepted the position of draftsman in the Machinery Department of the Toledo, Wabash, and Western Railroad, located at Springfield, Illinois. Being single, he sought lodging and found a most suitable place to board at 909 South Fifth. That happened to be the residence of Page Eaton and his family. In that house he met Lelia Anna Eaton and married her on October 3, 1878.

Promotions came rapidly for this capable young man. He advanced to Chief Draftsman, Mechanical Engineer, Erecting and Machine Foreman, Foreman of Machine Shops, General Foreman of All Shops (with 500 men under his control), General Foreman of Division Roundhouses and finally Assistant Master Mechanic. He resigned from the Wabash line in November of 1885 to work for another railroad. After several moves, he went to St. Paul, Minnesota, on January 16, 1891. In that city he became the Master Mechanic for the St. Paul & Duluth Railroad. When the Northern Pacific took over that company, Brooke remained as Master Mechanic. Nevertheless, a few years later, he became Superintendent of Machinery and Equipment for the Iowa Central and the Minneapolis and St. Louis Railway.

John F. Wallace, Chief Engineer of the Isthmian Canal Commission, interviewed Brooke in Chicago on September 28, 1904. As a result, the dynamic Theodore Roosevelt,

President of the United States, sent George D. Brooke, Jr., to Panama—at a salary of $375 per month in gold—as one of the first engineers so chosen to plan and construct the great canal and railroad across the Isthmus. Even his thesis had hinted at this tremendously-important appointment. Back in 1875, Brooke had researched "The application of steam to raising water." He also studied "The peculiar properties of a pumping engine." He was an innovator and a thinker and could manage large numbers of workers. Roosevelt liked Brooke extremely well. Both were Freemasons and had a close fraternal tie.

Brooke arrived in Panama on October 17, 1904, and left only after the Army took over five years later. Under the most trying of climatic conditions, he had supervised construction there as Chief of the Bureau of Machinery and Equipment. He advanced to this position on June 1, 1905. On September 1 that year, he became Superintendent of Motive Power and Machinery. When Secretary of State Elihu Root paid a visit to the Canal Zone in September, 1906, Brooke received appointment to the committee which had charge of all the ceremonies, inspections, and consultations. Then on November 15, 1906, Brooke had another responsibility added to his shoulders. He became Superintendent of the Panama Railroad Company and supervised the maintenance of its rolling stock and floating equipment. Hence, when President Theodore Roosevelt came down to see the Canal in November of 1906, Brooke escorted him on much of his tour.

In addition to his several other assignments in Panama, Brooke "carried to conclusion the task of designing, installing and operating the plants necessary to light the Canal Zone with electricity and to operate the drills on the Culebra cut with compressed air." Some drills used steam, too. As soon as Army officer G.W. Goethals became the Chief Engineer in February of 1907, he asked Brooke to remain so he could finish the Canal. Brooke agreed and helped plan the Gatun Locks and those at Miraflores and Pedro Miguel. He was the senior engineer on these projects.

Brooke's health had suffered in the malarial tropics, and he resigned his posts on September 22, 1909. At his farewell dinner held at the Tivoli Hotel in Ancon, Canal Zone, on Saturday, October 8, none other than Dr. W.C. Gorgas appeared and spoke about "The Chase of The Wily Mosquito." Engineer Brooke had been one of the great leaders who helped dig the "Big Ditch." They all knew and respected Brooke. The famous Gorgas, as sanitary engineer, had eliminated yellow fever by destroying the cause of the dreaded disease: the mosquito. But he could not stop the malaria which had struck Broke. To a newspaper in Phoenix, Arizona, Brooke confided that "five years is as long as an American should live in that climate unless he decides to remain there permanently."

Upon retirement from the Panama Canal project, the Brookes returned to Minneapolis where they resided at 2742

Bryant Avenue South. From this base, they traveled extensively. However, George's health declined; his physician ordered him to stop smoking cigars. After a severe illness, G.D. Brooke died on April 10, 1922, at the age of 69. He received a Masonic funeral with burial in Lakewood Cemetery.

His widow, with "the aching void of Dad's loss" ever with her, remained at the family residence until death claimed her, too, on July 13, 1927. She had suffered with heart trouble for some years. Her obituary proudly recounted the fact that her father, Page Eaton, had helped construct the home later purchased by Abraham Lincoln.[26]

Yes, the Brookes had associations with two of the greatest American Presidents: Abe Lincoln and Teddy Roosevelt. What delightful stories they must have been able to tell their children around the cheery evening fire. Lelia, as a young girl, had seen the renowned Lincoln in Springfield. George had rubbed elbows with General George Washington Goethals, the chief engineer of the Canal; Dr. William Crawford Gorgas; Teddy Roosevelt; and many others.

Brooke had a son, William Stacy Brooke, who held membership in Canal Zone Lodge at Ancon, Panama. He did not take a demit from that body until December 13, 1924, when he wished to join a Symbolic Lodge in St. Paul, Minnesota, where he had removed three years previously. This fact proves that he remained in the Canal Zone to work long after his father had gone. William had entered Panama in 1907 where he secured a draftsman's position, perhaps in his father's office.

This was the home of G. D. Brooke's family at Culebra from 1905 to 1909. Photo in the collection of Marshall D. Brooke; copy by Winfred (Doc) Helm.

In November of 1906, Pres. Theodore Roosevelt visited the Canal Zone to inspect the Panama Canal. He was the first President in 117 years to leave the jurisdiction of the U. S. He journeyed across the Isthmus with his Masonic Brother, George D. Brooke, Jr., the Superintendent of the Motive Power and Machinery Division. Here, Pres. Roosevelt is shown in a white suit on the rear of an observation car with Brooke just to the right and slightly behind the President. From *National Magazine*, XXVI, 135 (Apr., 1907). It is Brooke's own copy, owned by Marshall D. Brooke. Copied by Winfred (Doc) Helm.

G.D. Brooke's farewell dinner party took place in the Tivoli Hotel at Ancon in Canal Zone. In this hotel, Pres. Roosevelt had stayed during his visit to the Canal. *National Magazine*, XXVI, 141 (Apr., 1907). Copy by Winfred (Doc) Helm.

In this dining room at the Tivoli Hotel on October 8, 1909, G.D. Brooke was honored with a farewell dinner. Dr. W.C. Gorgas attended and spoke on "the Chase of the Wily Mosquito." *National Magazine*, XXVI, 141 (Apr., 1907) Copy by Winfred (Doc) Helm.

Note George D. Brooke sitting on bottom row, fifth from the left. Col. W. C. Gorgas is in middle row, second from the left. *National Magazine*, XXVI, 137 (Apr., 1907). Copy by Winfred (Doc) Helm.

References

17 Power, ed, *History of the Early Settlers*, 280-281; Page Eaton to Mr. & Mrs. Geo. D. Brooke, Springfield, Ill., May 7, 1893, MS., Coll. Mr. & Mrs. Marshall D. Brooke, 127 S. Forest Ave., Palatine, Ill., 60067.

18 Marriage License No. 567, Sangamon County Clerk's Office; *Illinois Daily Journal*, May 27, 1852, p. 3, c. 2.

19 *Daily Illinois State Journal*, July 21, 1856, p. 2, c. 4.

20 *Ibid*., Jan. 6, 1857, p. 2, c. 5.

21 *Builder of Lincoln's Home: Page Eaton* (Harrogate, Tenn.: Lincoln Memorial Univ. Press, 1962).

22 *Illinois State Register*, Dec. 21, 1899, p. 8, c. 1.

23 *Ibid*.

24 *The Illinois State Journal*, Apr. 22, 1901, p. 6, c. 3.

25 Power, ed., *History of the Early Settlers*, 280-281; U.S. Census 1850, Springfield, Sangamon Co., Ill., pp. 110 A and B.

26 Brooke MSS., in the possession of Page Eaton's great grandson, Marshall Dillon Brooke, R. Ph. Proof of George D. Brooke's residence in Springfield with the Eatons is found in *Springfield City Directory and Sangamon County Record Biographical and Statistical, 1877-78* (Springfield: M.G. Tousley & Co., Jan., 1877), 17, 33.

This "Lady's Work Box" measures 9 3/8" long, 6 3/4" wide, and 4 1/8" high. It contains one thousand, two hundred and nineteen pieces which are inlaid over the original walnut taken from the Lincoln Home. Written on the bottom of the piece are these words: "Inside material, [lum]ber from A. Lincoln's Home, Springfield, Ill." It is owned by Luann Elvey who holds the copyright to this photo taken by Thomas C. Elvey. Note the removable inside tray.

Roll, Ludlum and Brayman

No previous publication has adequately described the renters who occupied the cherished Lincoln home for a year and a quarter while the jubilant Lincolns sojourned in Washington, D.C., and other places. And, it may not be amiss to repeat in this chapter the well-known story of another construction man who has long been connected with repairs made to the Lincoln homestead in 1849-50. Here, however, for the first time, this builder's life will be examined and followed right down to the date of his death. Thus, his biographical sketch presented in these lines is not merely a twice-told tale afterall.

Restorations and corrections were perhaps required because the Eighth-Street property had been rented out for awhile. Yet, the proud owners may have merely wished to remodel the interior slightly and spruce it up. Five years had passed since the Lincolns had acquired this house, and repairs at this time could well have been dictated as a result of the normal wear and tear inflicted by the Dressers and the

John Eddy Roll (1814-1901), a friend of Lincoln's since 1831, did plastering and brickwork in the Lincoln home during 1849 and 1850. From the six walnut doors which Roll received from Lincoln as part payment, he made furniture that remained in his family as mementos.

Lincolns who both had growing children. Anyway, part of the improvements centered upon the antiquated fireplaces and their replacements.

The enterprising workman who utilized the ancient square and compasses in his labors inside the Lincoln property was John Eddy Roll. He started life June 9, 1814, in Green Village, Morris County, New Jersey, the son of William and Mary (Eddy) Roll. His father taught school in that tiny hamlet but moved westward with his family, arriving in Sangamon County, Illinois, on June 7, 1830. Within a few weeks, they removed from the farm home of a great-uncle, Jacob C. Roll, where they had found temporary shelter, and took up housekeeping in Sangamo Town.

Young Abraham Lincoln drifted unannounced into Sangamo Town the next spring to fabricate a flatboat on the Sangamon River for the would-be-businessman Denton Offutt who planned to establish a produce trade route from central Illinois down the Mississippi to New Orleans, the "Land of Dreams." Charles Broadwell had already opened a steam sawmill at Sangamo Town, and there existed plenty of free government timber on the nearby sections as yet uncleared. Thus, Offutt, quite naturally, decided to build his boat at this particular spot southeast of New Salem.

Roll recalled rather humorously his first sight of the incredible Abraham Lincoln. "He was tall, gaunt and bony," Roll remembered, "and as homely as he has ever been pictured to be. He was the rawest, most primitive looking specimen of humanity I ever saw, his clothing all too scant for him. His trousers lacked four or five inches of reaching the ground, usually with the legs stuffed into big rawhide boots. At this time he wore an old roundabout far too short for him, so that when he stooped over he showed four or five inches of his suspenders. His hat, drab colored, small crown and broad brim, was well worn. He was a general favorite of all with whom he came in contact, and with his story telling and genial spirit he soon made friends and became the life of the village."

Abe Lincoln quickly informed the curious villagers that he had been sent to boss the manufacture of a flatboat, "for which he was to receive $15.00 per month for his services." Not having any better prospects, John E. Roll immediately approached the tall friendly foreman and applied for a job. "He hired me," Roll declared, "and I made the pins for the boat." These vital wooden pins held the heavy boat together.

As soon as he finished his labors on the flatboat, Roll migrated east into Springfield where he learned the trades of plasterer and brick mason. After mastering these useful crafts, he eventually became a master builder and contractor. He joined The Springfield Mechanic's Union on October 3, 1839. It was because of his building skills that Roll once again sold his services to Lincoln. Upon Lincoln's final return to Springfield (March 31, 1849) from his single term in Congress, he decided that his prized home should have some extensive refurbishing.

Having been elected to the United States Congress, Abraham Lincoln had determined to take his spouse and family (Robert and Eddie) with him to Washington, D.C., for the first year. Therefore, being a thrifty home owner, he

$198 57/100 No. 7985

Received of the AUDITOR WARRANT on the TREASURER of the State of Illinois for One hundred & Ninety Eight Dollars and fifty Seven cents, in full, for an appropriation made Ass by the Genl Assembly Dec 1846 & 1847

SPRINGFIELD, Mar 6/47

C Ludlum

Cornelius Ludlum signed a receipt on March 6, 1847, for his $198.57 payment from the Legislature. As usual, he did not put a period after the "C" for his first name. Auditor's Receipt Book, 1845-1849, MS., Illinois State Archives.

needed to lease his house at Eighth and Jackson for at least enough cash to pay the taxes and upkeep while away from Springfield.

On October 23, 1847, Lincoln succeeded in negotiating a contract with one Cornelius Ludlum, 41, and a native of either New York City or New Jersey, who agreed to pay him ninety dollars rent, "in quarter yearly payments," for the privilege of living in the Lincoln residence one year, beginning November 1, 1847. Lincoln prudently reserved the right to use "the North-up-stairs room, during the term, in which to store his furniture." At the time of this agreement, Ludlum already had been in Springfield for at least five years.[27]

Although he touched the lives of numerous political figures and helped to influence history, practically nothing has previously been told of Cornelius Ludlum. As early as 1835, Cornelius resided in Morgan County (certainly Jacksonville). According to the census that year, he was between 20 and 30 years of age; had in his family one female between 10 and 20; one female between 20 and 30; and another female between 40 and 50.[28] Four years later, he aspired to public office and ran for Morgan County Treasurer. In an election held on August 5, 1839, he lost by a narrow margin in a three-man race but carried Jacksonville where he lived.[29] He seems to have had a penchant for financial management. When Harmony Lodge No. 3, A.F.&A.M., was first established in Jacksonville, Ludlum became its Treasurer.[30]

Upon being questioned by a U.S. Census taker in 1840, Cornelius Ludlum declared that his household consisted of: 1 male under 5 years of age; 1 male between 10 and 15; 1 male (himself) between 30 and 40; two females under 5; one female between 10 and 15; and one female 20-30 (his wife). Furthermore, he boasted that he fitted into the category of a "learned professional engineer" who also engaged in manufacturing or the trades. One member, he revealed, also dabbled in agriculture, perhaps meaning himself or his son who was between ten and fifteen. Such statistics seem to indicate that Ludlum still manufactured bricks or did masonry work. More importantly, however, this census establishes the fact that Ludlum already had become a railroader.

Ludlum and Murray McConnell had been appointed agents on the Northern Cross Railroad between Jacksonville and Meredosia, an important port and ferry on the Illinois River. Yet on January 4, 1841, both agents, through their State Senator, claimed that they were not "capable of managing, repairing or running the locomotive, and will be under the necessity of employing an engineer at considerable expense." Ludlum and McConnell prayed for monetary assistance from the Illinois General Assembly which had assumed control of the financially-troubled line.[31]

Evidently, the Legislature turned a deaf ear to their pleas for monetary relief to engage a professionally-trained railroader. Perhaps the Solons learned that Ludlum had already taught himself to operate the engines. Samuel Willard, who had then been a student at Illinois College in Jacksonville, recalled later that the engineer on the train which ran from Jacksonville to Meredosia was none other than Cornelius Ludlum. Furthermore, Willard declared that Ludlum was a careful man and an excellent operator. He often rode the cars as a passenger while Ludlum handled the throttle of the engine. Willard vouched that this engineer watched the iron-clad wooden rails with the keen observing eye of an eagle. As soon as he spotted a loose iron strap (called a snakehead),

This painting of Major General Mason Brayman hangs in the Old State House at Springfield, a building that he knew well. Photo courtesy of Ill. State Hist. Lib.

he stopped the puffing engine immediately, jumped down with his hammer and repaired the defect before the deadly iron band could spring up and run through the floor of a car and kill or injure an unsuspecting passenger.[32]

By March 25, 1842, the Northern Cross Railroad had extended its eastern terminus to Springfield. It proudly announced that its cars were at last "running on this road from the Illinois River to Springfield, leaving the river every Tuesday, Thursday, and Saturday, morning, and returning every Monday, Wednesday, and Friday." At Meredosia, passengers could make steamboat connections for St. Louis and arrive there in twenty-three hours after leaving Springfield.

So, it was at this time that C. Ludlum moved his family to Springfield to operate the train on this line. Being in the capital, Ludlum could also lobby the Illinois State Legislature more easily for additional benefits on behalf of this railway. Exactly when he arrived, we do not know, but he voted in Springfield on August 1, 1842. From a study of the poll book for that election, we know that Ludlum was a Democrat since he declared himself for Governor Thomas Ford and Lt. Gov. John Moore. Those were the only two he bothered to favor at the polling place. He continued to support the Democratic ticket in 1844 and 1846. On August 3, 1846, he even cast his vote for Peter Cartwright—and thus against Abraham Lincoln—in the Congressional race for Representative from the Seventh District.

In the Capital City on June 6, 1844, Ludlum was proposed for membership in The Springfield Mechanic's Union by Thomas Lewis, a shoemaker, and James C. Sutton, a carpenter and joiner. Although he won election at that meeting, he did not actively participate in this educational institution. Actually, he did not show up and sign the Constitution until April 3, 1845. On that date he carefully dipped his pen into the inkwell and wrote his name, "C Ludlum"—without a period—and set down in writing that he was by trade a mason. (All of his known signatures have no period after the "C" for Cornelius.) From this important entry in the Minute Book, we know that he was not only a speculative mason but also an operative mason.

The Ludlums lost two young children while living in Jacksonville—Cornelius, Jr., ten months of age, died July 19, 1838—and Andrew Todd. Following these tragedies, Cornelius' wife, Lavinia Maria Ludlum, died in Springfield on January 18, 1847, as a result of consumption. According to her obituary, she was in her 36th year and came from Rahway, New Jersey.[33]

Tiring of a constant financial loss on the Northern Cross Railroad, the Illinois General Assembly by an act approved February 16, 1847, ordered the Governor, Augustus C. French, to sell this line to the highest bidder. Then, on the 28th of that same month, the Legislature—which referred to him as a resident of Sangamon County—appropriated $198.57 to Ludlum for his relief.[34] Since 1844, Ludlum, with the aid of a partner, had rented the Northern Cross from the State of Illinois for $160 per month. So, this state payment certainly related to Ludlum's operational expenses in some manner. Since he remained in Springfield, C. Ludlum may have continued to work for this rail line even after its sale to other individuals.

Despite the passing of his wife and a bleak financial outlook, Cornelius Ludlum leased the Lincoln home on October 23, 1847, a fact which indicates that he still had other members of his family living with him. He had probably met Lincoln through their mutual interest: railroads. The Honorable A. Lincoln had always held a deep fascination for internal improvements—railroads and canals. In his very first published political address (March 9, 1832), Lincoln had announced that "Time and experience have verified to a demonstration, the public utility of internal improvements."[35] And during his four terms in the Illinois General Assembly, he labored mightily for the Northern Cross Railroad. In fact, he was probably its best friend in the Legislature.

Cornelius Ludlum and at least his children (Edward, Thomas, and Julia), moved into the Lincoln home by November 1, 1847. Evidently, however, Mr. Ludlum soon thereafter fell upon harder times and needed cheaper and smaller accommodations. He paid three-months' rent—$22.50—to Lincoln's agent, John Irwin & Company, on February 1, 1848, and that ended his short stay in the famous Lincoln residence. Yet, he had legally signed a one-year lease and still remained liable for the remainder of the contract period.

Rather than allow the financially-troubled Ludlum to suffer the pains of default to a renown lawyer who might sue for the money, a fellow member of the Craft came to his assistance: Mason Brayman. Being a speculative mason, too, his name fitted him perfectly. A clever, struggling attorney-at-law, Mason Brayman presented a striking appearance. He stood 5' 11" tall, had dark brown hair and blue eyes. On February 1, 1848, he settled his little family into the comfortable Lincoln house. His household consisted of four: himself, 34 years of age; his wife, Mary, 31; one young daughter, Ada, about nine; and a “Miss Emily,” called “Aunty,” who was either a relative or an employee that assisted with housekeeping.

Mason Brayman, son of Daniel and Anna (English) Brayman, had been born in Buffalo, New York, on May 23, 1813. He started his career as an editor of the *Buffalo Bulletin*, then shifted into law. At that city in 1836 he took to wife Mary Williams. He then practiced in Michigan where their daughter Ada was born. Sometime later, he brought his family to Springfield, Illinois. Although a prominent Democrat, Brayman and Lincoln quickly developed a cordial relationship. They sometimes practiced law together. As early as July 5, 1839, Lincoln and Brayman defended Alexander Pope Field, a Whig and the Secretary of State, in a suit before the Sangamon County Circuit Court. Thus, their friendship began soon after Brayman reached Springfield.

Since legal clients proved to be very scarce, Brayman busied himself with other tasks which paid money, or promised to pay money. After Gov. Thomas Ford (1842-1846), a Democratic colleague, suggested that the laws of Illinois then in force needed to be assembled into one volume, Lawyer Brayman commenced this monumental task in April of 1844. Through the Governor's influence, both Houses passed a joint resolution on January 18, 1845, formally authorizing Brayman to make the compilation. By a bill approved March 3 that year, the lawmakers allowed him $800 for his large tome. Having a ready facility with words, Brayman completed the writing on September 25, 1845. He had produced a volume of 749 pages with an additional sixteen pages of introductory material. It wisely contained notes and an index. On the front page appeared his name, M. Brayman. Its title page read: *Revised Statutes of the State of Illinois* (Springfield: Wm. Walters, 1845). Sad to relate, though, the payment did not follow the book's publication and distribution.

By necessity, Brayman occupied his mind and hands with other matters. Being a noteworthy and active Baptist lay leader, he joined others of this denomination in founding the Peoria Female Seminary. He became a trustee when the incorporation papers went into force on March 1, 1847, by act of the Legislature.

Still no money came to Brayman from the State of Illinois for his *Revised Statutes*. Because his law practice earned him only a precarious living, he sought outside employment. He turned once more to his lively pen. When the Illinois Constitutional Convention assembled on June 7, 1847, in the Hall of the House of Representatives at the State House, Brayman showed up there at 3 p.m. to cover the proceedings for the St. Louis *Union*. Delegates voted to invite reporters to take a seat within the bar which they promptly removed to make more room. Brayman thus had a choice spot to observe history in the making. However, his journalist's income stopped when the Convention finished its work on August 31, 1847.

By closely watching his expenditures, Brayman thought that he could afford to rent the Lincoln house and took over Ludlum's lease on February 1, 1848. But he was not flush with money. When his first quarter's payment fell due on May 1, Brayman neglected to give it to John Irwin & Co. In fact, he did not discharge this obligation of $22.50 until August 4. Fortunately for him, nobody pressed him for the requital. In writing to his sister Sarah on June 8, 1848, Mason advised her that his was "about the happiest family you ever saw." He then made a brief mention of the Lincoln home to her. "We have an excellent house and garden—with plenty of cherries and currants, and peaches growing—with vegetables of my own raising," he boasted with justifiable pride. Thanks to this missive, we learn that the

Lincolns did have fruit trees in their backyard but with enough room left over to spade up a vegetable garden. Brayman reiterated to his sister that he still practiced law. From a later letter, however, we can state for certain that his legal practice suffered greatly from a lack of paying clients.

Brayman confidently informed his relatives back in Buffalo that he felt certain of winning election as Clerk of the Second Grand Division of the Illinois Supreme Court, a lucrative position in Springfield at the State House. But when the votes were counted on September 4, 1848, he discovered that he had lost to his worthy opponent, William B. Warren, a Past Grand Secretary of the Grand Lodge, A.F. & A.M. Having corresponded for years with fellow members and distributed the printed proceedings, etc., Warren's name was extremely well-known to hundreds of voters living in the Second Grand Division which encompassed thirty counties in Central Illinois. Warren polled 13,466 to Brayman's 12,601, a difference of only 865, or less than 29 votes a county.

When the Lincolns appeared back in Springfield on October 10, 1848, Brayman still owed six months' rent—due October 31. Not until November 1 would the original lease expire. Lincoln had no legal claim upon his house until that date.

Be that as it may, the Lincolns still required lodging until November 1 came. They made a sentimental choice and carted their suitcases and trunks over to the Globe Hotel where they had lived, loved and taken their meals for many months following their marriage on November 4, 1842. It fronted on the north side of Adams Street, midway between Third and Fourth. They would have noted a big change in these quarters. J.M. Allen had greatly enlarged the hotel in 1846, making it a T-shaped building and much more commodious than before. A Mrs. Chatterton boarded there at the time the Lincolns returned from the Nation's Capital. She happily recalled the tall amiable Congressman ambling "up and down the hotel dining room shaking hands with everyone." Among those living in the thirty hotel chambers were several women who had no man to tote the wood up to their rooms. Each accommodation possessed a fireplace and stove. With his characteristic kindness and thoughtfulness, the Hon. A. Lincoln carried the heavy wood from the cord outdoors to the ladies' bedrooms. Said Mrs. Chatterton, "He was common, like some one that is poor." Nor was he merely campaigning for votes; he was not running for reëlection, and women could not vote anyhow.

Somehow, Mason Brayman scraped up $50 in cash on November 18 and called upon Congressman Lincoln to pay six months rent: from May 1 through October 31. While the Lincolns had been absent, Brayman had spent five dollars of his own money repairing the fence. Upon being told of this expenditure, Lincoln gave him $5 credit, making the remittance equal $55. While transacting this business, Lincoln decided to let Brayman rent the house for another quarter, that is, from November 1 1848, to February 1, 1849. With his own hand, Lincoln wrote out a receipt to Brayman for a $55 payment, and since the back rent amounted to only $45, he advanced the congenial renter a credit of $10 on the next quarter's obligation.

Brayman thereby remained living in the Lincoln home, while the Lincolns continued boarding at the Globe. Near the end of November in 1848, however, Congressman Lincoln kissed Mary and the two boys goodbye and departed for Washington, D.C., in order to attend the last session of the 30th Congress. Mary, Robert, and Eddie kept their downtown room at the Globe. That wise arrangement would be easier for Mary than having her beg to stay with one of her three married sisters in town. Then, too, Lincoln probably did not want his wife and children to live by themselves in the house at Eighth and Jackson during the lonely, frigid winter months.

Mason Brayman proudly apprised his father that business had "improved very much" and he was "doing now much better than formerly." Still, he had not received his money from the State of Illinois for compiling the *Revised Statutes*. He decided to wait no longer. On December 29, 1848, he stomped into Governor Augustus C. French's office on the second floor of the State House and filed a formal complaint. Not only was French a fellow Democrat, he was also a fellow member of the Craft. Needless to say, a special act whizzed through the General Assembly, and Gov. French signed it on February 10, 1849. Within minutes—before the ink on this enrolled law had even dried—

$800.) No. 464

Received of the AUDITOR WARRANT on the TREASURER of the State of Illinois for Eight hundred dollars and ——— cents, in full for an appropriation made me for Superintending the printing of the Revised Statutes &c.

SPRINGFIELD, Feby 10/49 M. Brayman

On February 10, 1849, Mason Brayman signed an Auditor's receipt, No. 464, for his pay as compiler of the *Illinois Revised Statutes*. Auditor's Receipt Book 1845-1849, MS., Illinois State Archives.

Brayman hurried into the Auditor's office on the first floor, signed a receipt, and picked up his $800 warrant.

That large fee saved Brayman's financial life. "The appropriation I got from the State last winter, and what I have gained in business," Brayman explained to his father and mother on July 1, 1849 "enabled me to get clear, and to live with my little family in comfortable circumstances until now."

With his single Congressional term finished, Abraham Lincoln came back to Springfield by himself on March 31, 1849. Brayman and his family had probably remained in the Lincoln home until the returning Congressman actually arrived. Mary and the boys certainly waited for Father Abraham in the Globe Hotel.

Not until May 9, 1849, did Brayman take his final rent

payment to Lincoln. Although the original document has pieces missing and the exact figures cannot be ascertained, Lincoln probably charged him only $12.50—one quarter's rent minus the ten dollars credit allowed back on November 18. That would have been for the period November 1, 1848, to February 1, 1849. Lincoln signed the receipt again in his own hand.

Mason, Mary, and Ada Brayman then took occupancy of a "little quiet home," near the Lincoln house, at the northwest corner of Eighth and Edwards. Both families enjoyed being close friends. By diligent efforts, Brayman's law practice increased to the point that by November 4, 1850, he owned $1,500 worth of real estate—his home, no doubt. Then, he obtain a most profitable appointment. In 1851, he and William H. Bissell (later, Governor of Illinois from 1857-60) became solicitors for the Illinois Central Railroad. Now, it was possible for Brayman to repay Lincoln for his earlier generosity in relation to the back rent on the house at 8th and Jackson. On October 3, 1853, Counselor Lincoln informed Solicitor Brayman that "Neither the county of McLean nor any one on it's [sic] behalf, has yet made any engagement with me in relation to it's suit with the Illinois Central Railroad, on the subject of taxation." "I am now free to make an engagement for the Road," offered Lincoln. He asked Brayman to "count me in."

Brayman quickly dispatched his personal check for $250 to Lincoln, thus retaining him as an attorney for the

I.C. That case alone brought Lincoln a fee of $4,800. And "Old Abe" continued to be a lawyer for this important line. His and Brayman's ways crossed often after that.

It so happened that on Monday, February 27, 1860, Lincoln and Brayman both found themselves staying at the Astor House in New York City. Lincoln had traveled east to speak at Cooper Union that evening, and Brayman lingered in that city of high finances to transact railroad business. That morning Brayman called at Lincoln's room to greet him. While they visited, "a Black Republican" and his committee appeared "to take [Lincoln] up Broadway." "Ancient Abraham," as Brayman called him politely in jest, presented Brayman to this partisan delegation with a humorous word of caution. "To these unsophisticated heathens," as Brayman jokingly termed them, Lincoln divulged that Brayman espoused the Democratic cause—not the Republican. Later that day, Lincoln and Brayman took dinner together. While these two old friends sat eating, a group of Lincoln's admirers approached the table. The former railsplitter and farmer "turned half round and talked 'hoss' to them—introduced me as a Democrat, but one so good tempered that he and I could 'eat out of the *same rack, without a pole between us*.'" After that homespun remark, the visitors roared with laughter. Subsequently, Brayman went to listen as Lincoln gave the speech which helped make him President of the United States.

Brayman continued to support Father Abraham and vice

versa. Soon after the black war clouds rolled over the North from the smoking guns at Fort Sumter, Mason Brayman accepted a Major's commission in the 29th Infantry Regiment, Illinois Volunteers. At the time he left the Army four years later, he held the high and coveted rank of brevet Major General.

Following the Civil War, Brayman practiced law and acquired political office. From 1867 to 1873, he sat on the Board of Trustees for the infant University of Illinois. He also edited a newspaper in Springfield, Illinois, before leaving for Wisconsin. President Ulysses S. Grant, a Republican, later named him Governor of Idaho Territory where he ruled from 1876 to 1880.

About 1885, he went to Kansas City, Missouri, to live with a daughter and son-in-law, Mr. and Mrs. Theodore Gowdy. Although far removed from Springfield, Illinois, Brayman never forgot his fraternity ties there. While living at 1734 Phelps Avenue, he wrote his Lodge on December 6, 1892, saying, "Very soon, the shadow will fall. I may not meet my brethren again here, *yet*, 'in the House *not* made with hands.'"

At 81, after a long and fruitful life, General Brayman died on February 27, 1895, in Kansas City—thirty-five years to the very day after he heard Lincoln utter his famous address at Cooper Institute. He, too, had lived and died in the Lincoln legend.

The dreadful Bright's disease killed him. After a local

memorial service, his tired, spent body rode the rails one last time back to picturesque Ripon, Wisconsin. That city had been home to him and his wife for several happy years. The mournful train bearing his remains whistled its way into Ripon on the evening of March 1. Immediately, the casket was tenderly borne to the Baptist Church where a loyal honor guard of G.A.R. veterans stood over it throughout the long chilly night. All during the morning hours next day, visitors from far and near passed the bier to pay their last tearful respects to Maj. Gen. Brayman. At 2 p.m. on March 2nd, Dr. E.H. Merrell and Rev. E.R. Clevenger conducted the funeral, assisted by Col. Geo. W. Carter of the local G.A.R. Post. At the conclusion of this religious ceremony, the General's body was gently interred, with full military honors, beside his beloved wife, Mary (Oct. 8, 1816-Feb. 19, 1886), in the SE 1/4 of Lot 20, Western Division, of Hillside Cemetery.

Both the General and his lady were Baptists and had transferred their letters to the local church of that denomination in Ripon on November 14, 1872. Abraham Lincoln, too, had attended the Baptist Church as a youth. But the Braymans shared more than a religious experience with the great Lincoln. They had shared an important segment of his life in Springfield, Illinois, and elsewhere. Yet the Braymans lie buried so far from the Land of Lincoln that the connection has long been forgotten. In fact, his few biographical sketches list the General's burial place as Kansas City.[36]

Now, back to the fascinating tale of Cornelius Ludlum.

During the spring of 1849, he fled from Springfield. His railroad endeavor had perhaps petered out. For whatever reason, he chose to be an adventurous Forty-Niner and threw in his lot with a wagon train headed west to California where gold had been discovered the previous year. He left his remaining family members in Springfield. From Independence, Missouri, he wrote home on May 12, 1849, saying that he was traveling in an overland caravan which consisted of 100 wagons and 150 men. They intended to proceed by the southern route, Ludlum thought. By July 2, the gold hunters had reached Santa Fe. From there they went on by the Gila Trail and into Santa Cruz.

As frequently happened to numerous gold seekers with a practical head, Ludlum finally stopped chasing the elusive, precious, yellow metal and continued into San Diego where a friend reported seeing him. At the time he joined The Society of California Pioneers, Ludlum, himself, vouched that he had reached California on December 15, 1849.

Within a year, he drifted on up to bustling San Francisco. In that beautiful Golden Gate City by the Bay he became acquainted with Joseph W. Farrington and formed a partnership with him called Farrington & Ludlum. They operated as commission merchants at 99 California Street. When a man by the name of Wier fell into debt to them during the latter part of 1851, they took over his brickyard on the south side of Mission Creek. Although Ludlum knew this business well, he did not operate it. Instead, Farrington

& Ludlum leased "Wier's Brick Yard" on November 4, 1852, to Bellows & Webster for $100 per month. Farrington & Ludlum continued their commission business. Farrington considered himself a "broker" anyway.

A state census enumerator counted and recorded Cornelius Ludlum in San Francisco in August of 1852. Cornelius revealed to this inquiring official that he still counted Illinois as his permanent residence and earned his living as a merchant. According to directories, Ludlum did not continue his partnership with Farrington very long after this date.

Having made money in San Francisco and saved a sizeable amount of his earnings, Ludlum change his mind, returned to Illinois, and gathered up his remaining family so they all could live in San Francisco. From available records, it seems that he brought back Edward, Thomas Budgley and Julia. This time, however, Cornelius took the easier water route out to California: by way of the Isthmus. (Julia Ludlum later married L.D. Stephens in San Francisco.)

After returning to San Francisco with his children, Cornelius Ludlum continued working as a merchant with a dwelling at 223 California Street. Then, just prior to the opening of the Civil War, he changed occupations. He secured appointment as "wharfinger" (overseer) on the Broadway Wharf and took up a residence at 92 Stevenson. Ludlum certainly knew the transportation field, although the sea would have been a new experience for him. By the end of the war, Ludlum was collecting tolls for the California Steam Navigation Company on the same wharf. By 1869, however, he returned to being a wharfinger on this dock. Again, he changed jobs about 1875, becoming a weigher on the wharf for the California Pacific Railroad Company with his office on Broadway Street. At long last, Ludlum had returned once more to employment with a railway, even if it happened to be in the very twilight of his variegated life. He retired from his labors about 1877 while living at 2251 Mission.

The Grand Architect of the Universe summoned him from this mortal life on October 23, 1878, at the age of 72 years. Ludlum succumbed exactly thirty-one years to the very day after he had signed the lease agreement with A. Lincoln. The old fortune-seeker had actually discovered his hard-sought-after "gold" when he settled down at the Golden Gate beside the blue Pacific way back in 1850. Even in life, his venturesome soul had climbed "halfway to the stars" in that wonderful cosmopolitan city which has so inspired writers of song and story. He must have loved it greatly, because once he saw it, he remained there to the end. No more drifting about in search of a better life. What a treat for a man raised on the Atlantic Coast to be able to buy fresh seafood directly from the honest fishermen's catch-of-the-day proudly displayed along the wharf.

Back on August 2, 1860, Ludlum had joined California Lodge No. 1, F. & A.M., in San Francisco. As soon as

Secretary Geo. T. Grimes learned of this death, he informed the Master who summoned the officers and members to assemble at 1 p.m. on October 24, Thursday, in King Solomon's Hall, on the northwest corner of Montgomery and Post, and conduct a Masonic funeral for "our late Brother, CORNELIUS LUDLUM." Following this ancient ritual, they escorted his body to Calvary Presbyterian Church, at the northwest corner of Geary and Powell, for "religious services."[37] Thus, we can assume that Ludlum had been a Presbyterian. Unfortunately, his place of burial has not been discovered. In 1914, the Board of Health ordered all burials to be removed from the city limits of San Francisco.

Following the residencies of Ludlum and Brayman as renters in his home, A. Lincoln sought the tradesman's skills of John E. Roll. This old Sangamo Town friend plastered walls and whitewashed four ceilings, plus the kitchen, filled in fireplaces and remade the hearths. The Hon. A. Lincoln much preferred stoves to inefficient open fires where most of the heat went up the chimney. He took an interest in scientific matters and kept up with the latest developments.

On April 23, 1849, Roll presented his bill to Lincoln for $26.60. (The date of this already-accomplished remodeling indicates Brayman did not remain in the house after March 31, 1849. If Brayman had occupied the home for an additional quarter, he would not have left until April 30.)

Always a shrewd bargainer, Lawyer Lincoln gave Roll six walnut doors as part payment on his account. It is extremely doubtful if these valuable doors had been taken out of the Lincoln dwelling. Roll did not charge for any carpentry work. Rather, the very usable doors had probably been accepted by Barrister Lincoln as part of a legal fee. Barter often transpired at Springfield in those days of scarce cash. Paul F. Sullivan, a ranger at the Lincoln home, and this author believe that there simply were not six doorways which could have been replaced by arches or new doors put in for old ones. At that time, the residence stood only a story and a half in height. However, there were two sleeping chambers upstairs.

Again, on March 30, 1850, Roll finished whitewashing two additional rooms at Lincoln's place and submitted his charges: two dollars. Lincoln finally paid this rather small bill on August 30, five months late. It is possible that the Lincolns wished to spruce up their home and forget a sorrowful and tragic event which had transpired there on February 1, 1850. On that black day, the Lincolns lost their youngest son, Edward Baker Lincoln, not yet four years of age. Chronic consumption snuffed out his precious life.

After building about one hundred houses and doing extensive remodeling work around town, John E. Roll changed his occupation. He plunged into the real estate business to sell or rent some of the houses which he had constructed. Later, he sold boots and shoes, too. He died

March 30, 1901, and his remains were taken out to Oak Ridge Cemetery where they found a place in this scared burial spot, not far from the immortal Lincoln. John Eddy Roll had helped write a chapter or so in the fascinating life history of Lincoln in Illinois.[38] And like Brayman and Ludlum, Roll also died on an anniversary date of his connection with A. Lincoln. He succumbed fifty-one years to the exact day after having whitewashed the Lincoln residence. History is indeed more fascinating than fiction.

Addendum

By October 1, 1847, A. Lincoln had engaged E.G. Johns, a local house and sign painter, to repaint his house on Eighth and Jackson. He signed a note for up to $10 worth of [linseed] oil to be purchased from Converse & Priest. Johns needed this ingredient to thin his paint. From this evidence, we know that the Lincoln home was freshly painted when Ludlum rented it. (Basler, ed., *The Collected Works*, I, 405, 420.)

References

27 Basler, Pratt, and Dunlap, eds., *The Collected Works of Abraham Lincoln*, I, 406-407.

28 Illinois State Census of Morgan County, 1835, p. 59, MS., Illinois State Archives. As usual, his name is badly misspelled.

29 Illinois Election Returns, XXXIX, 46, MS., Illinois State Archives.

30 Ludlum must have become a Mason prior to 1840. He assisted in founding the Grand Lodge of Illinois at Jacksonville and during the first few meetings acted as Grand Pursuivant and Grand Marshall. On October 21, 1840, he was appointed the Grand Tyler of the Grand Lodge. He also served with the Committee on Finance. In 1842, C. Ludlum became Senior Warden of Harmony Lodge No. 3 at Jacksonville. He kept his membership as a Master Mason in No. 3 until he left the State of Illinois in 1849. *Reprint of the Proceedings of the Grand Lodge of Illinois 1840-1850* (Freeport, Ill.: Journal Print., 1892), 7, 9, 11, 73. *Sangamo Journal* (Springfield), Oct. 30, 1840, p. 2. c. 7.

31 U.S. Census 1840, Jacksonville, Morgan Co., Ill., p. 19, 1. 19; *Journal of the Senate of the Twelfth General Assembly of the State of Illinois* (Springfield: Wm. Walters, 1840[-1841]), 133.

32 Samuel Willard, "Personal Reminiscences of Life in Illinois—1830-1850," *Transactions Illinois State Historical Society,* XI, 83-84 (1906).

33 *Illinois State Register*, Mar. 25, 1842, p. 2, c. 6; Sangamon County Election Returns, Springfield Poll Books, Aug. 1, 1842, Nov. 4, 1844, and Aug. 3, 1846, MSS., IRAD, University of Illinois at Springfield; Minute Book of The Springfield Mechanic's Union, 108, 132, MS., Illinois State Historical Library; *Illinois State Register*, Jan. 22, 1847, p. 3, c. 3; *Sangamo Journal*, Jan. 28, 1847, p. 3, c. 2. Thanks to Betty F. Pine of the Jacksonville Public Library for aid.

34 *Laws of the State of Illinois Passed by the Fifteenth General Assembly* (Springfield: Chas. H. Lanphier, 1847), 109-111; *Private and Special Laws of the State of Illinois, Passed by the Fifteenth General Assembly* (Springfield: Chas. H. Lanphier, 1847), 150-151, 189.

35 Basler, Pratt, and Dunlap, eds., *The Collected Works of Abraham Lincoln*, I, 5.

36 *Ibid.*, I, 407; Brayman's physical description is from his Masonic record; he was initiated in Springfield Lodge No. 4 on Nov. 30, 1846, passed Jan. 15, and raised Jan. 29, 1847; he was Chaplain, Junior and Senior Warden but then in 1850 became High Priest of Royal Arch Chapter No. 1 in Springfield; he joined Apollo Commandery, Knights Templar, at Chicago in 1856 and helped organize Elwood Commandery in Springfield; he remained a Mason until he died. Records of Lodge No. 4, Masonic Temple, Springfield, Ill. *Laws of Illinois* (Springfield: Walters & Weber, 1845), 369; *Private and Special Laws of Illinois* (Springfield: Chas. H. Lanphier, 1847), 166; Constitutional Convention Journal, 2 vols., MSS., Illinois State Archives; Mason Brayman to his sister, Sarah, Springfield, Ill., June 8, 1848, Bailhache-Brayman Coll., MSS., Illinois State Historical Library; Election Returns 1818-1850, p. 579, MS., Illinois State Archives; *Illinois State Register*, Oct. 13, 1848, p. 2, c. 5; Octavia Roberts, "We All Knew Abr'ham," *The Abraham Lincoln Quarterly*, IV, 25 (Mar., 1946); James T. Hickey, *The Lincolns' Globe Tavern* (Springfield: Ill. State Hist. Lib., 1964); *Executive Record*, V, 182, MS., Illinois State Archives; *Laws of Illinois* (Springfield: Chas. H. Lanphier, 1849), 31-32; Auditor's Receipt Book 1845-1849, No. 464, MS., Illinois State Archives; Mason Brayman to his father and mother, Springfield, Ill., Jan. 7, July 1, 1849, Bailhache-Brayman Coll.; Mary Brayman to brother and sister, Springfield, Ill., July 2, 1849, *ibid.*; U.S. Census 1850, Springfield, Sangamon Co., Ill., p. 117 B, 11. 21-24; A.T. Andreas, *History of Cook County, Illinois* (Chicago: A.T. Andreas, 1884), 175; Basler, Pratt and Dunlap, eds., *The Collected Works*, II, 205; Brayman letters, Chicago Hist. Soc.; *Jour. Ill. State Hist. Soc.*, XLIX, 213-214 (Summer, 1956); some of Brayman's correspondence was with Wm. H. Bailhache, his son-in-law, of Springfield who in 1858 had affiliated with Lodge No. 4, A.F. & A.M.; Executive Record, VIII, 334, MS., Illinois State Archives; *Illinois State Journal*, Feb. 28, 1895, p. 1, c. 6; this obituary mentions Brayman's residence in the Lincoln home but has the wrong time, saying it was while Lincoln was President; Samuel M. Pedrick's collection of Ripon family genealogy in Ripon College Archives; *The Ripon*

Commonwealth, Mar. 1, 1895, p. 3, c. 6; *The Ripon Free Press*, Mar. 5, 1895, p. 1, c. 4; and Hillside Cemetery Records, MS., Ripon, Wis.

37 *Illinois Journal,* May 30, 1849, p. 1, c. 5; Sept. 19, 1849, p. 3, cc. 3-4; Jan. 24, 1850, p.3, c. 1; May 20, 1850, p. 2, c. 2; California Census of 1852, San Francisco Co., Pt. II, 152, microfilm, Ill. State Hist. Lib.; *In the Supreme Court of the State of California, John C. Bower and Joseph W. Farrington, vs. H.P. Coon et als.* (San Francisco: M.D. Carr & Co., 1869); Lease from Farrington & Ludlum to Bellows & Webster, Nov. 4, 1852, MS., and various San Francisco directories, California Historical Society, San Francisco; Members' Index, and Mortuary Records, 1865-1884, I, 83, MSS., The Society of California Pioneers, San Francisco; J.M. Guinn, *History of the State of California and Biographical Record of Coast Counties, California* (Chicago: Chapman Pub. Co., 1904), 1353; records of the Grand Lodge, F. & A.M., of California, San Francisco; *San Francisco Daily Alta California*, Oct. 24, 1878, p. 4, c. 3, p. 8, c. 3.

38 Garda Ann Turner, ed., "John E. Roll Recalls Lincoln," *Lincoln Herald*, LXII, 103-105 (Fall, 1960); Power, ed., *History of the Early Settlers*, 627-628; John Linden Roll, "Sangamo Town," *Jour. Ill. State Hist. Soc.*, XIX, 153-160 (Oct., 1926-Jan., 1927); Pratt, *The Personal Finances*, 87. Although John E. Roll's account book existed when Harry E. Pratt did his research, it has now dropped from view. Fortunately, J.L. Roll reproduced some of the entries in his article as did Pratt in his book. Minute Book of The Springfield Mechanic's Union, 14, MS., Illinois State Historical Library. Eddie Lincoln's death is recorded in the U.S. Census 1850, Mortality Schedule, Sangamon Co., Ill., p. 787, 1. 23, MS., Illinois State Archives.

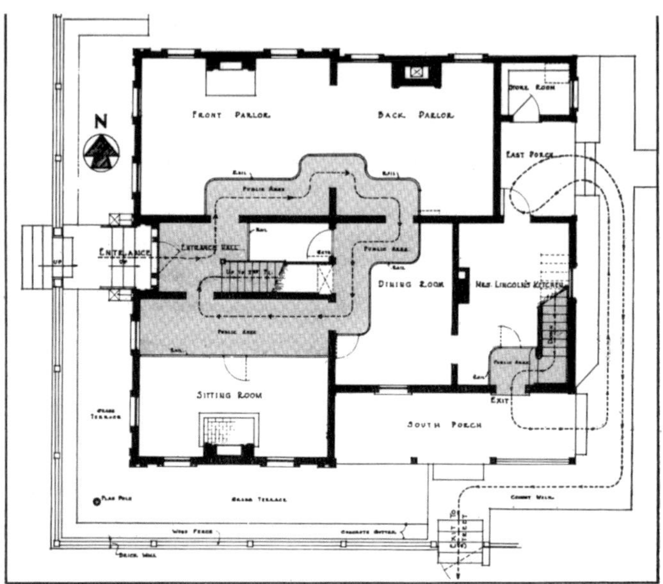

First Floor Plan of the Lincoln Home

Shaded sections on both drawings indicate the public areas.

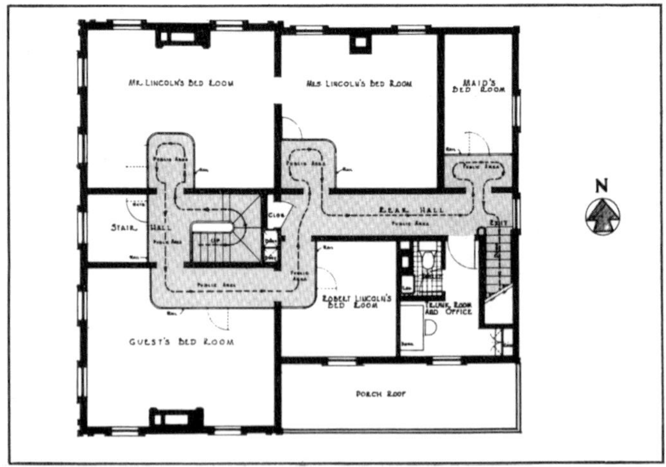

Second Floor Plan

Expansion of the Lincolns' House

On September 18, 1854, Mary (Todd) Lincoln sold eighty acres of farm land which her father, Robert Smith Todd, had given her back in 1844. For this tract—described as the East Half of the Southeast Quarter of Section 12, Township Fifteen North, Range Six West of the Third Principal Meridian, located in Curran Township of Sangamon County, Illinois—Wife Mary received $1,200 from Robert Anderson, a local man. So, it is quite possible that she herself decided to enlarge the home at Eighth and Jackson with her own money.

Without question, though, Mary discussed the remodeling program with her husband to seek his advice and consent. She had enormous respect for his keen judgment and sagacious perception. In fact, she told Congressman Lincoln by letter in May of 1848 that "good persons generally agree" with you. Historians who think that Lincoln knew nothing of the rebuilding program until it was actually done, have been led astray by a tale repeated by James Gourley, a reputable shoemaker from Pennsylvania who lived just behind the Lincolns. Upon reaching home—probably on May 30 or June 7, 1856—from a long stint on the judicial circuit, Lawyer Lincoln supposedly sauntered up to a neighbor on the sidewalk, with a twinkle in his bluish-grey eyes, and asked in feigned seriousness, "Stranger, do you know where Lincoln lives?" After a slight pause, Lincoln continued, "He used to live here."

One must evaluate this delightful story for what it is—a humorous joke, the likes of which Lincoln loved to act out to an appreciative audience. But trouble begins immediately when some writer takes it at face value without seeing the intended jest. Gourley may never have heard the conversation in person, although he probably did. He and his wife, Lucy, with their six youngsters, resided on the northwest corner of Ninth and Jackson, adjoining the Lincoln property. Cobbler Gourley often befriended Mrs. Lincoln while her tall Circuit Rider practiced law far from home.

This we do know as a fact. As soon as suitable spring weather came in 1856, the Lincolns began remodeling the east wing of their home to make it a full two storeys in height. "Mr. Lincoln has commenced raising his back building two stories high," reported Mrs. John Todd Stuart of Springfield to her daughter, Bettie, on April 3, 1856. "I think they will have room enough before they are done," Mrs. Stuart quipped with playful malice, "particularly as Mary seldom ever uses what she has."

John Henry Schuck (1830-1913) assisted in the expansion of the Lincoln Home at Eight and Jackson streets in 1856. At that time he worked as a lumberman for George L. Huntington who owned a lumberyard located opposite the Great Western Railroad Depot, near Tenth and Monroe, and very close to the Lincoln residence at Eighth and Jackson.

DANIEL HANNON, Cairo.] [THOS. A. RAGSDALE, Springfield.

HANNON & RAGSDALE,

BUILDERS,

THIRD STREET, BETWEEN ADAMS AND MONROE,

SPRINGFIELD.

Springfield residents saw this advertisement for the popular building firm of Hannon & Ragsdale in the *Springfield City Directory for 1857-58* (Springfield: S. H. Jameson & Co., 1857). It had been solicited by the compiler about 1856. Readers must be aware that directories are about a year old when they first appear on the market.

By working long hours, the construction men must have had the back building at least under roof by May 10, because on that date Mrs. Lincoln purchased wallpaper from John Williams & Company. She certainly would not have had need for paper if the building were not secure from storms and showers. There has always been much speculation as to how the structure was expanded, but Neighbor James Gourley—a man fifty-one years of age at that time—vouched in writing that the carpenters took "off the roof" to "raise the house." This testimony should answer that question permanently.[39]

After the rebuilding project reached fruition, Mary Lincoln, boasting to her half-sister in Lexington, Emilie (Todd) Helm, wrote on February 16, 1857: "You will think, we have enlarged our borders, since you were here."[40] Of course, the house would have been finished for several months prior to this joyful announcement by Mary.

Two local men, Hannon & Ragsdale, whom one newspaper termed "architects and builders," handled this major construction project at a cost of $1,300.[41] Be that as it may, Daniel Hannon, Sr. (whose last name previous writers have misspelled) and Thomas Allen Ragsdale identified themselves only as "builders" and "carpenters" and had their establishment on Third Street between Adams and Monroe.[42] Nevertheless, in those days most carpenters and bricklayers were referred to as "architects and builders"—witness this same descriptive appellation being connected to the name of Page Eaton by the same newspaper.

However, Hannon & Ragsdale seem to have exhibited little or no personal supervision of their journeymen carpenters who spliced the studs to form a full top storey of the expanded house. In the early 1950's the State of Illinois dismantled part of the Lincoln home to make repairs and strengthen the aging framework. While this vital restorative work went on, Richard S. Hagen observed that "the methods used in joining the 1856 work to the 1839 structure would dismay a good carpenter. For example, odd pieces of wood were indiscriminately nailed together for studding, showing the carpenter to have felt that work which would be covered with lath and plaster could be done in any fashion."[43]

Back in 1839, the Eatons had constructed the Dresser home with sills, joists and interior woodwork fashioned from the beautiful native walnut. They selected oak, sawed in various widths, for the floors, and split hickory, prepared in the same manner, for the lath.[44] But contrary to the statement made by Hagen in 1955, the Carpenters Eaton did use black walnut for the siding. When the National Park Service scraped the precious boards all the way down to the bare wood in 1976, this author personally examined the original siding on the ninth of August. He immediately discovered that the ancient siding boards of the original 1839 structure had been cut from solid walnut, yet they measured only three-eighths of an inch in thickness.

Where absolutely necessary, skilled craftsmen inserted new lumber wherever needed in 1976, and then the exterior of the home received three coats of brown paint, the color preferred by Abraham Lincoln for his house so many years ago.[45] Superintendent Albert W. Baton did everything in his power to make the Lincoln home resemble the original residence as known by Abraham Lincoln and his neighbors in 1860.

Besides Hannon & Ragsdale who planned and supervised the expansion, what men actually did the 1856 carpentry when the remodeling took place at the Lincoln home? One additional person—a fraternal brother of Hannon's—can at last be identified as a result of new research by this present author. The *Illinois State Register* for Saturday, March 8, 1913, page three, columns two and three, recalled John Henry Schuck as "a personal friend of Abraham Lincoln and [one who] helped build the Lincoln homestead at Eighth and Jackson streets." Of course, the editors meant the 1856 expansion, since Schuck did not come to the United States until the summer of 1847 as a young man of seventeen years.

He had been born in Heidelberg, Germany, on March 1, 1830, the son of John Schuck, a cabinetmaker by trade. After serving an apprenticeship of two and one half years under his father, John Henry fled Germany to escape military conscription. After a long rough sea voyage of thirty days, he finally landed in New York City during the summer of 1847. From there he continued his odyssey inland to Chicago where he followed his carpenter's trade until 1848. (Note, again, the young and tender age of skilled craftsmen laboring alone and far from home.)

In 1848 he removed to Springfield, Illinois, and secured employment as a cabinetmaker. But with the discovery of gold in California, J.H. Schuck rode horseback to the mines the following year. Not finding his fortune at the spot now called Placerville, John reverted to his skillful trade of woodworking. He even repaired wagons and did other odd jobs for cash. At last in 1851, he gave up this area of the country and returned to Illinois and took up residence at Middletown in Logan County. Yet one year later, he came back to Springfield and reëstablished himself as a cabinetmaker.[46]

Being gainfully employed once more and twenty-two years of age, Mr. Schuck took to wife Mary Elizabeth Lightfoot on July 25, 1852.[47] A daughter of Henry F. and Mary T. (Jones) Lightfoot, she was the same age as Schuck, having been born the very same year that her parents arrived in Sangamon County.[48] Both John and Mary resided in Springfield when they asked the Reverend Mr. Robert E. Guthrie—a Methodist Episcopal minister and an active Mason—to marry them.[49] It was perhaps this preacher who gave the example which caused Schuck to join the Craft.[50]

Finding—unfortunately—that full-time cabinet making confined him indoors for long hours and seemed detrimental to his health, Schuck gave up this occupation in 1854 and joined the lumber firm owned by George L. Huntington. A sketch of Schuck in Wallace's history of Sangamon County relates that he began as a salesman. His new boss would have taken an active interest in Schuck's well being, since Huntington belonged to the same Lodge.[51]

Huntington, a Democrat, had been born in Northampton, Massachusetts, on August 26, 1811, and migrated westward to Springfield in 1840 where he entered the drygoods business with Virgil Hickox. Later, he established a huge lumberyard. He played the flute and led the first Springfield orchestra. In addition, he directed the Philharmonic Association, organized in June of 1860. One of the managers of this group was none other than John G. Nicolay who later became Abraham Lincoln's private secretary.

Huntington's death came on May 26, 1873, and his funeral was conducted by the Rev. F.M. Gregg, Rector of the Episcopal Church. Those mourners who followed his body to Oak Ridge Cemetery on the 28th formed the largest funeral cortège ever seen by the reporter who covered the services for Huntington. One editor termed him an "honorable and conscientious man."[52] A most successful entrepreneur by 1860, Huntington had amassed $25,000 worth of real estate, a personal estate of $10,000, and he kept three Irish servants in his household to do the heavy chores. At that particular time, his son, C.L. Huntington, 19 years of age, served as a Midshipman in the United States Navy.[53]

After he commenced his career with Huntington, John Henry Schuck listed himself as a lumberman. He lived on Second Street, near Canedy.[54] His exact duties at the yard are unknown now, but he still considered himself a cabinetmaker, too. A census taker in 1860 put him down as a "clerk" which in those day could even denote an administrator.

Previous to the first edition of this book, Lincoln literature never described Hannon and Ragsdale. Yet, both deserve recognition because of their interesting and important contributions to the building history of Illinois.

Daniel Hannon, Sr., was born in Charlestown, Massachusetts, in 1810. In that city he grew up and "received the benefit of a liberal education." Early in life, he chose "architecture" as his profession, meaning the building trade. In Charlestown he married Welthea Ewell, a native of Massachusetts and a year older than himself. By 1840, the Hannons had gone west to Lawrence County, Illinois, but they did not long tarry there. Shortly, they went on to Springfield, the capital city. In all, they raised six children: Daniel, Jr.; Mary E., who married B.F. Parker of Chicago; Horace A.; Lucy, who married George T. Cushing of Dubuque, Iowa; Charles; and Eva, who married G.W. Johnson of Dubuque, Iowa.

Thomas Allen Ragsdale was born October 2, 1812, near Keysburg, Logan County, Kentucky, a son of the Reverend Frederick Ragsdale, a Baptist minister who had emigrated from Virginia. Unfortunately for his family, the Rev. Ragsdale died just two years after the birth of Thomas A. In January of 1834, Thomas A. Ragsdale came to Springfield with an older brother, Daniel, and a sister, Mary. Daniel Ragsdale then married Eliza E. Bell in Springfield on November 3, 1836. And the very next day, Thomas A. Ragsdale married Dorcas Ann Bell. For the record, it would appear that these brothers married sisters. Descendants later told that the Bell girls came from Montgomery County, Maryland. Mary Ragsdale became the bride of Deriandus Sampson on September 5, 1838.

George L. Huntington (1811-1873) married Hannah L. Forbes of Boston. Upon coming to Springfield in 1840, both joined the Episcopal Church. Thus, they knew the Rev. Charles Dresser very well. George served as Alderman from the Third Ward of Springfield during 1856, 1857 and 1858. In 1861 and 1862, he won election as Mayor. Photo from the Illinois State Historical Library.

At some time during the 1840's, Daniel Ragsdale formed a partnership with Daniel Hannon under the name of Ragsdale & Hannon. Both advertised themselves as house joiners and carpenters. They kept their shop on Third Street, near the Globe Hotel—the place Abraham and Mary Lincoln set up housekeeping immediately after their marriage on November 4, 1842. Therefore, the Lincolns had long known these carpenters when they sought to expand their home in 1856. Thomas A. Ragsdale must have hammered and sawed as an unnamed member of the firm. Daniel Ragsdale resided on South Seventh Street. Hannon kept house in the "Edwards Addition," which is where they continued to dwell for a number of years. This would have been Spring Street, near Jackson.

For some reason, things went badly for Daniel Ragsdale. His lots were sold for back taxes in 1838; he and his wife began operating a boarding house the following year but declared bankruptcy in 1842. Next, he disappeared for awhile. By necessity, Daniel Hannon reorganized the firm taking in Thomas A. Ragsdale and switching the firm's name to Hannon & Ragsdale.

In reply to the questions of a census taker in 1850, both Daniel Hannon and Thomas A. Ragsdale declared themselves carpenters. Hannon reported real estate worth $450 and Ragsdale, $1,000. The latter had two daughters, Mary E., 11; and Anna E., 9. The Hannons still remained on Spring, near Jackson. The Ragsdales, on Monroe at the corner of Third.

Hannon occupied the secretary's chair of Sangamon Lodge No. 6, Independent Order of Odd Fellows, in 1852. T.A. Ragsdale entered politics and won election in 1854 as an Alderman from the Third Ward, thus helping to govern the City of Springfield in his spare time. Then, during 1855-56, Daniel Hannon was initiated, passed, and raised a Master Mason in Springfield Lodge No. 71, A.F. & A.M. He maintained his membership in this same lodge until the "Grand Architect of the Universe" summoned him from labor to refreshment.

By 1855, Hannon & Ragsdale had a growing clientele. In that year, they were erecting a three-story brick building on the west side of the Public Square. But sometime in 1856, Daniel Hannon left for Cairo, Illinois, in order to construct the "Springfield Block" and other buildings in that town which was growing rapidly because of the Illinois Central Railroad. That block alone would cost $50,000.

Although their partnership remained in tact, Ragsdale assumed a tremendous burden on his weakening shoulders. Now, he labored alone in Springfield to supervise their many construction projects. For instance, in 1856 they built two three-story brick stores on Washington Street along the north side of the Public Square, another store adjacent to it, and a two story store on Adams Street on the south side of the Square. In addition that year they fabricated numerous private residences: one each for Judge Samuel Hubbel Treat;

John J. Taylor; Robert P. Johnston; Mrs. Thomas Mather; and Dudley Wickersham.

Yet the largest and most costly structure begun that same year (1856) was a palatial mansion for Governor Joel Aldrich Matteson, a millionaire. While yet Governor, he purchased nearly a city block of land just opposite the Executive Mansion. It stretched south from the southwest corner of Fourth and Jackson for nearly an entire block towards Edwards and extended west to Third Street. Gov. Matteson hired the noted Chicago architect, John Mills Van Osdel (1811-1891) to draw the plans. This same man had made the drawings for the new Executive Mansion, just completed.

Under Van Osdel's supervision, T.A. Ragsdale put up this princely home, built of brick with a slate roof. At the end of September, 1857, Ragsdale completed this towered ostentatious mansion at a cost of $95,000—three times the price of the Executive Mansion. Since Matteson went out of office on January 12, 1857, he and his family had to reside in the St. Nicholas Hotel (southeast corner of Fourth and Jefferson) until their home was completed. Behind the main house stood a gardener's cottage, a greenhouse, barns, stables, etc. A brick wall ran around most of the estate. Unfortunately for architectural history, this huge show place was discovered to be on fire at 6:30 p.m. on January 28, 1873, while the temperature stood at six below zero. Water froze in the fire hoses; the magnificent home was completely destroyed. However, the out buildings remained unharmed. At the time of the conflagration, the Roswell E. Goodells resided in the main house. Goodell was a son-in-law of Matteson.

With all their building activities in 1856 and Hannon living down in Cairo, it is easy to understand why Hannon and Ragsdale's expansion of the Lincoln home exhibited sloppy workmanship where the studding were spliced, etc. This lone contractor probably had little time to supervise this rather small project on a day-to-day basis. Ragsdale generally had young carpenters boarding in his own home. These men, no doubt as apprentices, helped with the Lincoln home remodeling, too. In 1850, he had Robert V. Bell, perhaps his brother-in-law, and Simon Simonsson, a Norwegian, living with him. Both were carpenters.

After the Lincoln contract, Hannon & Ragsdale garnered one in 1857 to do work on the new Executive Mansion. Presumably, the Governor's residence had been completed under Gov. Matteson, so this job for the following Governor, Wm. H. Bissell, must have been rather minor alterations or repairs. Their labors cost the State of Illinois $190.82.

Hannon remained in Cairo to handle new and additional construction there. By a law approved February 9, 1857, the General Assembly incorporated The Cairo City Hotel Company. Among the fourteen incorporators were Daniel Hannon, Thomas Ragsdale, Ninian W. Edwards, William Butler, James C. Conkling, John Cook, Thomas H. Campbell and Benjamin F. Edwards, all Springfield investors. They received power by this act to "erect a hotel in the city of Cairo, Illinois." Despite this exuberant investment scheme, the firm of Hannon & Ragsdale Builders was dissolved by mutual consent on March 12, 1858. Nevertheless, work continued on this hostelry even though Cairo suffered a disastrous flood in June of 1858.

At Cairo in Alexander County, Daniel Hannon had been commissioned a Justice of the Peace on November 20, 1857. Then, on June 13, 1859, he obtained a Notary Public seal. From the time that Hannon went on the bench as a Justice of the Peace, he completely forsook the building business. In 1860, he gave his profession as "Magistrate," and revealed that his real estate held a value of only $3,000 with $300 in his personal estate. His son, Horace, at the age of seventeen was already a druggist and earning a living to help his father and mother. He worked for J.B. Humphreys & Company as a salesman and prescription clerk. Not long after the Civil War tore the Nation apart, Horace enlisted in the U.S. Navy on September 6, 1861, as a "first class boy." At the time that he left the service in January of 1866, he held the rank of Captain on a gunboat, having sailed with the Mississippi Squadron, fought in seventeen engagements, and been wounded at the battle of Greenwood. Like his father, Horace joined the Craft as a speculative mason and attended the Episcopal Church. After the war, he obtained the distributorship for White sewing machines in Southern Illinois, Kentucky, and Missouri.

Daniel Hannon was again commissioned a Justice of the Peace for Cairo on December 3, 1861. The next report we have of him is that he died in Cleveland, Ohio in 1863. His widow traveled up to Dubuque, Iowa, to join the household of one of her daughters. He son, Daniel Hannon, Jr., also resided in Dubuque at this time. And thus ends the saga of the builder, Daniel Hannon, Sr.

T.A. Ragsdale continued to prosper in Springfield. He formed a new partnership with a son-in-law, Wesley F. Kimber. They completed the beautiful St. Charles Hotel at Cairo, Illinois, and it opened toward the end of September in 1859 under the proprietorship of Ragsdale, Kimber & Co. It became quite famous when Brigadier General Ulysses S. Grant set up his army headquarters there and actually later it underwent a complete refurbishing and took the name Halliday House.

In 1860, Ragsdale professed himself now to be a builder—not a mere carpenter. He had amassed a fortune of $30,000 in real estate and settled $20,000 upon his daughter, Anna E., yet at home. Due to ill health, the partnership shifted to be called Kimber, Ragsdale & Company. As dry-goods merchants, they operated in the early 1860's on the west side of the Public Square and then went to 508-510 East Adams on the south side of the Square.

On November 12, 1876, at 7 p.m., Dorcas Ragsdale died at the family home on the southeast corner of Sixth and Edwards. "Consumption" had claimed another victim.

When Daniel Hannon & Thos. A. Ragsdale finished the 1856 remodeling of the Lincoln Home, it looked like this photo. John Henry Schuck and George L. Huntington assisted in this project. Photo taken in 1981 by Harry (Bud) Roberts.

She was only fifty-eight. Now a widower, Thomas struggled along with even worse declining health. He resided with a son-in-law, James Knickerbocker. Since he could no longer work at all, he dissolved his partnership with Kimber in 1883 and retired. Finally, at 8 a.m. on March 26, 1892, Thomas A. Ragsdale departed from this life at the age of 79. His body was borne to peaceful Oak Ridge Cemetery for burial two days later. He left two devoted daughters, Anna E. (Mrs. James W. Knickerbocker), and Mary E. (Mrs. W.F.

Kimber). At his death, Tom Ragsdale held membership in the First Methodist Episcopal Church of Springfield.[55]

Back in 1856, when Hannon & Ragsdale agreed to raise the Lincoln home and add a second floor, they had to have purchased their lumber from George L. Huntington's yard or they would never have procured the talents of Schuck. Although John Henry may never have carried hammer and nails or saw around the construction site at Eighth and Jackson streets, he somehow aided the Lincolns with their enlargement project. Perhaps he selected the necessary lumber and figured the amount of board feet required for the job, or perhaps he got out the needed millwork for the upstairs windows, etc. By chance, he may even have installed the millwork once it came from his plant; he enjoyed working out in the open air. In some manner, he "helped build the Lincoln homestead," as his obituary revealed.

Huntington's lumberyard sat opposite the Great Western Railroad Depot,[56] near Tenth and Monroe, and his planing mills (operating under the name of Huntington & Campbell) stood on Washington, near Tenth Street.[57] Thus, Hannon & Ragsdale would have had only a short haul to bring their building materials to the Lincoln home.

And there is yet another piece of corroborating evidence available to us. G.L. Huntington specialized in "pine lumber;" that was his big seller and almost the only wood that he advertised.[58] While restoring the Lincoln residence in the 1950's, Dick Hagen examined the interior parts long hidden from view and saw that Hannon & Ragsdale had "used northern pine for everything, including the upstairs millwork which was given artificial walnut graining."[59] All laths had been manufactured to a uniform size, too, and all the pieces of our building puzzle now fit together very tightly.

Probably right in the middle of the Lincoln construction job, Mary E. (Lightfoot) Schuck passed away. She succumbed at 8 a.m. on May 28, 1856.[60] Anyone who has ever lost a beloved wife will agree—as this author can attest—that John Schuck immediately tried to fill his lonesome days and longer nights with work. He may even have picked up his hammer and helped at this building site as much as possible when not at the lumberyard. We know for certain that John broke up housekeeping and went to board at Brown's Hotel on the north side of Adams, between Seventh and Eighth—very near to his work and the Lincoln Home.[61]

After sixteen months of mourning, John H. Schuck remarried. He got a favorable answer from his proposal to Katharina A. "Kate" Brucker, a daughter of Jacob Brucker and a stepmother named Mary Jane. The Rev. Mr. P.S. Staiger of the First German Evangelical Lutheran Church performed the nuptial ceremony at Mt. Pulaski, Logan County, on September 29, 1857, where the bride resided. She had been born in Denkendorf, Wurtemburg, Germany, on December 9, 1830, and emigrated to America with her parents in 1843, first living near Zanesville, Ohio, and then coming west to Mt. Pulaski three years later. The same age as Schuck, she did not survive her husband, either, dying at 3:50 p.m. on July 5, 1895, in Springfield.[62]

Very much unlike Abraham Lincoln in his politics, John Henry Schuck campaigned and won appointment as a delegate to the Sangamon County Democratic Convention held December 24, 1859.[63] These Democratic leaders later named him to represent them at the Congressional Convention which chose a candidate to run on their ticket for Congress.[64]

Nor was Schuck above using his considerable political and fraternal influence to his personal advantage. On August 18, 1860, a Saturday evening, John strolled downtown, perhaps after having a beer or two, and insulted a city policeman by the name of Robert G. McDonald, a carpenter who worked on the night police force. As soon as Schuck called him a "City Pup," a fight resulted. Immediately thereafter, Schuck found himself arrested and in jail. But he persuaded Police Magistrate Charles E. Dodge to give him a change of venue into a Democratic friend's court. There, Josiah Francis (Sept. 24, 1801-Jan. 26, 1889) not only let Schuck off but also fined the police officer three dollars. Needless to say, the Republican *Illinois State Journal* reported this affair quite fully to its partisan readers.[65]

At the time of President Abraham Lincoln's funeral in Springfield on May 4, 1865, each element of the marching columns required leaders and assistants. The procession formed on Washington Street (and other nearby ones leading into it) and then moved slowly east to Eighth Street. There, it turned down Eighth to Monroe and west on Monroe to Fourth. At that point, the cortège headed north and proceeded to Oak Ridge Cemetery. Local officials in charge of the parade arrangements picked Schuck as a Aide to the Marshal of the Seventh Division, commanded by the Hon. Harman G. Reynolds.[66] They certainly did not chose John for his devotion to Lincoln's Republican Party. No, the townsfolk must have remembered that he had been connected with the enlargement of the Lincoln home in 1856 and that he always had been a personal friend of the deceased.

By 1865, Schuck had saved enough money to enter into a partnership with William B. Baker. These two sold lumber and supplies until April of 1877 when Schuck struck off on his own. But in 1882 he took his son Charles into the business, calling it J.H. Schuck & Son. With diligent efforts, he founded the Retail Lumber Association of Illinois. On May 1, 1879, he took his place as a director of the First National Bank and engaged in many civic projects, such as the street railway. In addition, he organized the German-American Savings & Loan Association, formed to supply building funds for those who needed to borrow capital for construction.[67]

After a long fruitful life, full of honors and selfless service to his fellowman, J.H. Schuck died at 2:10 p.m. on March 7, 1913, in his family residence, No. 1043 South Fifth Street. His life had extended for eighty-three years. A daughter, Anna Haynes, and one son, Charles, survived him. Three sisters yet lived when Schuck passed away: Mrs.

Marie Damarin and Mrs. Johana Frorer of Lincoln, Illinois, and Anna Ortel of Lahr, Germany.[68]

His Masonic Brothers conducted Schuck's burial service on the tenth and accompanied the body to Oak Ridge Cemetery.[69] Although dead, his many contributions lived on after him. Washington Park, for instance, was one of his interests, and he had presided as President of this governing commission until November 10, 1890. And now—once more—his name is linked to that of Lincoln.

References

39 Deed Record, PP, 530-531; Justin G. and Linda Levitt Turner, eds., *Mary Todd Lincoln* (N.Y.: Alfred A. Knopf, 1972), 37; Emanuel Hertz, ed., *The Hidden Lincoln* (N.Y.: The Viking Press, 1938), 383; U.S. Census 1850, Springfield, Sangamon Co., Ill., p. 121 B, 1. 35 ff.; *Springfield City Directory. . .For 1855-6* (Springfield: Birchall & Owen, 1855), 16; Mrs. Stuart letter in John T. Stuart—Milton Hay Coll., MSS., Ill. State Hist. Lib., Springfield, Ill. Bettie Stuart in 1856 was away from home attending the Monticello Female Seminary at Godfrey. *Jour. Ill. State Hist. Soc.*, XLIX, 216-17 (Summer, 1956). Purchase account in Pratt, *Personal Finances of Abraham Lincoln*, 148

James Gourley petitioned Springfield Lodge No. 4 for membership on Jan. 13, 1851; was elected Feb. 13; initiated Feb. 13; passed Feb. 20; and raised a Master Mason Mar. 13. He held both Jr. and Sr. Steward's chairs. He also became a Royal Arch Mason in Springfield Chapter No. 1 between 1856-57. Died Mar. 26, 1874. Records of No. 4, MSS., Masonic Temple, Springfield, Ill. Received a Masonic funeral at Lodge hall on Mar. 28. *Illinois State Register*, Mar. 27, 1874, p. 4, c. 3.

40 Turner and Turner, eds., *Mary Todd Lincoln*, 48-49. Emily had been at Springfield in 1855.

41 *Daily Illinois State Journal*, Jan. 6, 1857, p. 2, c. 6.

42 E.H. Hall, comp., *Springfield City Directory. . .For 1855-6* (Springfield: Birchall & Owen, 1855), 17, 33. Daniel Hannon had been a member of the Springfield Mechanic's Union and clearly signed his name as "Hannon" on the Constitution. He also gave his occupation as "Carpenter." Minute Book of The Springfield Mechanic's Union, 6, MS., Illinois State Historical Library. His name is also put down as "Hannon" for his contracts with the State of Illinois. See footnote 55.

43 Richard S. Hagen, "What a Pleasant Home Abe Lincoln Has," *Jour. Ill. State Hist. Soc.,* XLVIII, 11 (Spring, 1955).

44 *Ibid*. Page Eaton recalled they used all "oak and walnut" in the home later purchased by Lincoln. Page Eaton to Mr. and Mrs. Geo. D. Brooke, Springfield, Ill., May 7, 1893. MS. Coll. of Mr. and Mrs. Marshall D. Brooke.

45 Wayne C. Temple, "Lincoln's Springfield Home in 1865," *Lincoln Herald,* LX, 16 (Spring, 1958).

46 Joseph Wallace, *Past and Present of the City of Springfield. . .* (Chicago: S.J. Clarke Pub. Co., 1904), 230-233.

47 Marriage Record, III, 56, Sangamon Co. Building, Springfield,

Ill.; *Illinois Daily Journal*, Tues., July 27, 1852, p. 3, c. 2. She sometimes went by the name of Elizabeth Mary.

48 Power, ed., *History of the Early Settlers*, 455-456.

49 A well-recognized cleric, Guthrie would later that year be appointed to the grand line of the Grand Lodge of Illinois, Ancient Free and Accepted Masons. In the Hall of the House of Representatives during the evening hours of October 7, 1852, Guthrie was formally installed as Grand Chaplain. *Illinois Daily Journal*, Oct. 9, 1852, p. 3, c. 1.

50 The following year (on February 21, 1853), Schuck petitioned Lodge Number Four in Springfield for membership. Voting Brothers of that Symbolic Lodge elected him to receive the Masonic honors on March 21. He was duly initiated on April 6, passed on April 18, and raised a Master Mason on May 26. In the years that followed, Schuck served his Brethren as Tyler, Junior and Senior Steward. Records of Lodge No. 4, A.F. & A.M., MSS., Masonic Temple, Springfield, Illinois.

51 Huntington was initiated Aug. 14, passed Nov. 6, and raised on November 22, 1848, in Lodge No. 4. *Ibid*. Along with Grover Ayres and Jackson A. Hough, Huntington sat on the Building Committee charged with constructing a Masonic Hall in 1853. *Illinois Daily Journal*, May 11, 1853, p. 3, c. 2. They built it on the northeast corner of Fifth and Monroe. It burned during the night of February 22-23, 1871. *Illinois State Journal*, Feb. 23, 1871, p. 3, c. 4. Huntington also served on the Finance Committee of Springfield Lodge No. 4, A.F. & A.M., with Charles W., Matheny and Addison Hickox. *Illinois Daily Journal*, Jan. 8, 1857, p. 2, c. 3.

Masonic research is difficult to do in Illinois because the Grand Lodge lost its records at Peoria by fire on Feb. 10, 1850, and again at Springfield in 1871. The Grand Lodge at the latter date had its records in the local Springfield Masonic Temple, too.

52 *Ibid.*, May 28, 1873, p. 4, c. 2; May 29, 1873, p. 4, c. 1.

53 U.S. Census 1860, Springfield, Sangamon Co., Ill, p. 569, 11. 15-27.

54 Hall, comp., *Springfield City Directory. . .For 1855*-56, 36.

55 William Henry Perrin, ed., *History of Alexander, Union and Pulaski Counties* (Chicago: O.L. Baskin & Co., 1883), 165, B 19; Illinois State Census 1840, Lawrence Co., V, 24; U.S. Census 1850, Springfield, Sangamon Co., Ill., p. 103 B, 11. 31-37; Springfield (Ill.) *Sunday Journal*, Mar. 27, 1892, p. 4, c. 3; Marriage Records, II, 23, 46, MSS., Sangamon Co. Bldg.; *Illinois Journal*, Aug. 22, 1849, p. 3, c. 1, Sept. 5, 1849, p. 4, c. 1; U.S. Census 1850, Springfield, Sangamon Co., Ill., p. 84 A, 11. 29-35, p. 103 B, 11. 31-37; *Illinois Daily Journal*, July 6, 1852, p. 3, c. 2; *ibid.*, Apr. 5, 1854, p. 3, c. 1; *Proceedings of the Grand Lodge of Ancient, Free and Accepted Masons of the State of Illinois* (Chicago: Chas. Scott, 1856), 108-109; *Illinois Daily Journal*, July 14, 1855, p. 3, c. 1; Perrin, ed., *History of Alexander...*, B 19; *Springfield City Directory For 1857-58* (Springfield: S.H. Jameson & Co., 1857), [102]; *Daily Illinois State Journal*, Jan. 6, 1857, p. 2, cc. 5-6; Ragsdale's obituary cited above says he did Matteson Mansion; Van Osdel claimed the Matteson Mansion in his writings; Turner and Turner, eds., *Mary Todd Lincoln*, 50; *Illinois State Register*, Jan. 29, 1873, p. 4, cc. 3-4; *Illinois State Journal*, Jan. 29, 1873, p. 4, c. 3; U.S. Census 1850, Springfield, Sangamon Co., Ill., p. 84 A, 11. 29-35; Auditor's Receipt Book, 1856-59, p. 104A, MS., Illinois State Archives; *Private Laws of the State of Illinois, Passed at the Twentieth General Assembly* (Springfield: Lanphier & Walker, 1857), 327-328; *Daily Illinois State Journal*, Mar. 19, 1858, p. 2, c. 5; Executive Record, VII, 215, 572, VIII, 457, MS., Illinois State Archives; U.S. Census 1860, Cairo, Alexander Co., Ill., p. 10, 11. 10-14; *Daily Illinois State Journal*, Sept. 13, 1859, p. 3, c. 2; John Y. Simon, ed., *The Papers of Ulysses S. Grant* (Carbondale: S.I.U. Press, 1969), II, 181, 290; U.S. Census 1860, Springfield, Sangamon Co., Ill., p. 242, 11. 23-25; *Springfield City Directory 1877-78* (Springfield: M.G. Tousley & Co., Jan., 1877), 60,

83; *Daily Illinois State Register*, Nov. 13, 1876, p. 1, c. 4; W.F. Kimber married Miss Mary E. Ragsdale on Jan. 6, 1858, *Daily Illinois State Journal*, Jan. 8, 1858, p. 2, c. 4; U.S. Census 1880, Springfield, Sangamon Co., Ill., E.D. 229, p. 4, 1.7; *Springfield Sunday Journal*, Mar. 27, 1892, p. 4, c. 3; Burial Records, Block 7, Lot 108, MS., Oak Ridge Cemetery.

Daniel Hannon would have associated fraternally with Gov. Joel A. Matteson since both were Freemasons. Matteson belonged to Juliet Lodge No. 10 at Joliet, Ill., as early as 1842. *Reprint of the Proceedings of the Grand Lodge of Illinois 1840-1850* (Freeport, Ill.: Journal Print, 1892), 75. Thus, Hannon & Ragsdale would have had an inside track in obtaining the lucrative contract for building the Matteson Mansion. Matteson was a Democrat and a close friend of Senator Stephen A. Douglas. Thomas A. Ragsdale was perhaps a Whig; Daniel Ragsdale was. So, he would have known A. Lincoln politically.

56 *Illinois Daily Journal*, Jan. 2, 1851, p. 4, c. 3; B. Winters, comp., *Springfield City Directory, For 1857-58* (Springfield: S.H. Jameson & Co., 1857), 58.

57 Hall, comp., *Springfield City Directory. . .For 1855-56*, 20.

58 *Illinois Daily Journal*, Jan. 2, 1851, p. 4, c. 3.

59 *Jour. Ill. State Hist. Soc.*, XLVIII, 11 (Spring, 1955).

60 *Daily Illinois State Journal*, Wed., May 28, 1856, p. 2, c. 4.

61 Winters, comp., *Springfield City Directory, For 1857-58*, 78, 38.

62 Marriage License, County Clerk's Office, Lincoln, Ill.; *History of Logan County, Illinois* (Chicago: Inter-State Pub. Co., 1886), 636, 759; *Daily Illinois State Journal,* Oct. 6, 1857, p. 2, c. 3, July 6, 1895, p. 5, c. 5.

63 *Daily Illinois State Journal*, Dec. 22, 1859, p. 3, c. 2.

64 *Ibid*. June 11, 1860, p. 3, c. 2.

65 Aug. 25, 1860, p. 3, cc. 3-4. Josiah Francis was a Brother Mason, a member of Springfield Lodge No. 4.

66 *Ibid.*, May 4, 1865, p. 2, c. 5.

67 Wallace, *Past and Present of the City of Springfield*, 230-233.

68 *Illinois State Register*, Mar. 8, 1913, p. 3, cc. 2-3.

69 Records of Lodge No. 4, A.F. & A.M., MSS., Masonic Temple, Springfield, Ill.

Knud Olsen and the Lincolns

At some time between 1859 and 1861, Abraham Lincoln had need of a few repairs or improvements to his cherished home. He therefore contracted with a good friend, John Armstrong, to do the necessary carpentry work. A contractor and builder, Armstrong had been born in Chester County, Pennsylvania, on November 14, 1814. Like many others, he migrated out to Springfield, Illinois, where he arrived August 1, 1837—the same year Lincoln came to town. (Perhaps he came to work on the new State House.) He then married Chloe E. Abel on November 14, 1839, the anniversary of his own birthday.[70]

In due time, Armstrong established a carpenter shop in the alley located between Fifth and Sixth and Monroe and the Public Square. For living quarters, he secured a house that stood at what was then called 111 South Fifth—just opposite the Governor's Mansion.[71]

As his business expanded and grew more prosperous, Armstrong expressed a willingness to train young men in his own craft. One of those selected by him to be an apprentice carpenter was Knud Olsen who actually moved into the Armstrong home and resided there while learning this occupation. Another apprentice living with the Armstrongs at this time was George Homer from Maryland.[72]

During the Summer of 1860, John Adams Whipple of Boston took this picture of the Lincoln home (0-38). The south porch, shown here, had a trapdoor in the floor. This opening led to the basement which existed only under the front portion of the house. Here, Shaw developed his negative on August 8, 1860. Photo courtesy of Dr. Lloyd Ostendorf.

Knud Olsen had been born in picturesque Aust-Agder County, Norway, on November 10, 1838, the son of Ole Knudsen and Ingeborg Kirstine (Gjeruldsdatter) Olsen. There, he learned the trade of a miller but emigrated from his homeland in 1858. From Scotland, he worked his way by ship to Cuba and ended up in Delaware with a case of yellow fever. After getting out of quarantine, he moved over to Pennsylvania where he labored as a blacksmith and a carriage maker for four dollars a month. Looking for a better opportunity, Olsen went west to Springfield, Illinois, in 1859. Here, he met John Armstrong who agreed to teach him carpentry.

During the course of Olsen's instruction, John Armstrong was hired to perform some unknown wood work at the Lincoln home. It seems most logical that the Hon. A. Lincoln would engage this particular carpenter. Armstrong and Lincoln were political allies. Armstrong was Chairman of the Sangamon County Republican Convention and on January 12, 1860, organized the Lincoln Club in Springfield. He guarded the campaign funds as its Treasurer and confidently predicted that Lincoln would be the next President of the United States. When this prophesy came true, President Lincoln in 1861 appointed Armstrong the Postmaster of Springfield, a position he held until August 5, 1865. Upon leaving the Post Office, Armstrong quite naturally returned to the building trade. "Uncle John," as he was affectionately called, remained in Springfield until he died early on a Sunday morning, December 23, 1877, and was buried in Oak Ridge Cemetery. Armstrong had been severely ill for several weeks. He left a daughter, Lucye, who was married to C.H. Foster, a merchant at Pawnee, Illinois.[73]

William Shaw, a professional photographer of Chicago, took this view (0-34) of the Lincoln home on August 8, 1860. Shaw, 26 and born in New York, journeyed down to Springfield for this huge Republican rally. Dr. Lloyd Ostendorf acquired this original print with Shaw's imprint and the following notation: "After this picture was taken[,] Mr. Lincoln made a dark room out of the cellar for the photographer & stayed there with the operator during the process of the development." So, the Lincoln residence once served as a photo lab. Lincoln took a great interest in scientific matters and would have observed the process very carefully.

Evidently, Armstrong needed several days to complete the construction, because Olsen recalled that he "was sent there to work and got to know the Lincoln family." Such a statement indicates that the job lasted for several days. Otherwise, Olsen would not have had time to get friendly with the Lincoln household. Like his boss, Olsen campaigned for the Republican ticket and attended the party rallies where he yelled himself hoarse for the "Railsplitter." After election day—November 6, 1860—Olsen had the privilege of shaking Lincoln's hand and congratulating him at the State House where the President-elect stood receiving the well wishes of his supporters. In reply to a question about the difficult times facing the Nation, Lincoln said that "he thought it would be all straightened out without trouble when he got to Washington."[74]

With the additional carpenter work executed by Armstrong and his men, the Lincoln home should have been in fine shape when President-elect Lincoln rented it to Lucian Tilton, President of the Great Western Railroad, on February 8, 1861, for $350 per year. If any additional repairs were needed, Tilton agreed to make them. The Lincolns left for Washington, D.C., three days later, and the lease started to earn money for Lincoln on March 1 that year.[75]

On October 8, 1861, Knud Olsen took to wife Bertha G. Lund; the Rev. Dr. William M. Reynolds performed the religious ceremony.[76] Reynolds served as President of Illinois State University in Springfield—where Robert T. Lincoln once attended and where his father was a Trustee—and held the pastorate of the English Lutheran Church.[77]

Taken in 1920, before he left for California, this photograph shows Knud Olsen on the extreme right side. Left to right: Alma Christoferson Olsen, wife of Knud's son George; Holder Olsen, their son; George Olsen; Mabel Olsen, their daughter; and Knud Olsen. Of George and Alma's children, Holder had brown hair. Mabel was a blonde. Original photo owned by Bernice M. Bordeaux, Wallace, Michigan.

Olsen had evidently met his bride through one of her relatives who also sawed and hammered as a carpenter on the payroll of John Armstrong. Jacob Lund was his name.[78] But Miss Lund probably did not reside at Springfield in 1860. Rather, in that census year, she seems to have toiled as a house servant in the home of A.M. Haines of Galena, Illinois. Like the bridegroom, she too had been born in

Norway, on December 22, 1840, the daughter of Germanson and Engeber Lund. And her next-door neighbor in Galena happened to be none other than Ulysses S. Grant. Both Haines and Grant earned their livings as prosperous merchants there.[79]

Mr. Olsen heard the sad news of Lincoln's assassination while standing on the railroad depot platform at Macon, Illinois. Unfortunately, he did not get to view the President's remains at Springfield after the funeral train arrived. But his wife waited in line four hours to catch a glimpse of the murdered Commander-in-Chief's body as it lay in state at the Capitol.

Knud Olsen had one more connection with the Lincoln legend. In 1869, the National Lincoln Monument Association, a private organization, contracted with William D. Richardson of Springfield to erect the Lincoln Tomb in Oak Ridge Cemetery for $136,550. Richardson, who had submitted the low bid, was approximately 32 years of age and came originally from Connecticut. He arrived in Springfield during 1856 to work on the Great Western Railroad. *The Springfield Directory* later listed him only as a painter who boarded at the corner of Fourth and Edwards. Yet the Federal census assigned him no occupation whatsoever; most interesting, however, was the fact that he possessed $40,000 in real estate and had $15,000 in personal goods. At this time he had small experience for such a large undertaking, or so it would seem. He did not enter the construction business until about 1867; his most prominent job was the courthouse at Carlinville where he furnished the brickwork only.[80] Later, however, he blossomed out into a prominent contractor and even completed the new State Capitol. He had developed a paving technique, too. In the future, he would command the Fifth Regiment of the Illinois National Guard with the rank of Colonel.

Larkin Goldsmith Mead, Jr. (1835-1910) had won the contest for the design of the Lincoln Tomb and received his prize money of $1,000 on September 12, 1868. Strangely enough, though, Mead had trained only as a sculptor—not as an architect. To enter the lucrative competition, Mead (a resident of Florence) had simply hired an Italian architect to make the tomb design. This rather crude drawing Mead brought "to New York and had it re-drawn in my office by a French draughtsman," testified Peter B. Wight while he served as Secretary and Treasurer for the Board of Examiners of Architects in Illinois. Wight revealed this confidential information to Gov. John R. Tanner on March 10, 1899. Russell Sturgis, Jr., Secretary of the American Institute of Architects in New York City, drafted the blueprints for Mead. The "complete design" was badly garbled "when it went to Springfield," explained Wight from first-hand knowledge.

When the Monument Association discovered that Mead was no architect, the startled members suddenly realized that Mead could not oversee the construction. Yet they went ahead with his plans anyhow. (Twice it has been necessary to rebuild the Lincoln Tomb.)

Instead of going on as the supervising architect, Mead returned to his friendly little studio in historic and inspirational Florence, Italy. Lying on the beautiful Arno River, Florence boasts a proud heritage of unsurpassed artistic works from the Renaissance forward. Who would not be inspired by the tomb of Michelangelo in Santa Croce, the Cathedral of Santa Maria del Fiore, Ghiberti's bronze doors on The Baptistery, Michelangelo's New Sacristy for the Medici Family with its gorgeously carved tombs, the Uffizi Gallery, Palazzo Pitti, Michelangelo's "David," and the picturesque Ponte Vecchio, to mention but a few of its art treasures beyond price.

After Mead departed, ground was broken for the Lincoln Tomb on September 9, 1869. Over in Florence, Mead prepared to sculpt the Lincoln statue and the four proposed statuary groups depicting the various branches of the service during the Civil War: Navy, Infantry, Artillery, and Cavalry. He had garnered a most profitable contract for this artistic project to honor the memory of Abraham Lincoln.

Yet there exists a sincere doubt that Mead actually modeled the statue of Lincoln. At the time of its unveiling at the Tomb on October 15, 1874, a fellow artist living in Florence revealed by letter that Mead had not actually executed the work of art. No, S.M. Healy declared vigorously, Mead had merely hired two local Italian artists to make the statue.[81]

This revelation sounds truthful. We know, too, that Mead had previously paid Sturgis and others to draw the Tomb plans. Mead's record was, afterall, not impeccable, was it?

Knud Olsen helped carve and build the models used to cut the stone for the Lincoln Tomb in Oak Ridge Cemetery at Springfield, Illinois. William D. Richardson held the contract to construct this beautiful monument designed by Larkin G. Mead, Jr. and Russell Sturgis, Jr. the architect. Photo by Winfred (Doc) Helm.

No matter who did it, Mead's representation of President Lincoln is not an extremely great piece of art. It appears as stiff and cold as the bronze itself. Besides, it is not an outstanding likeness, either. Anyhow, after 1874, Mead never returned to the shores of the United States. As promised, though, the four statuary groups were eventually paid for, finished and shipped to the site of the Lincoln Tomb in Springfield, Illinois. The last one—the Cavalry ensemble, arrived in 1880. Each group of figures is an outstanding example of some artist's—or artists'—skill, knowledge and understanding. Every one appears to have frozen a small segment of an unnamed battle into solid bronze. Each man and animal is animated, and the viewer stands before these four groups tensely waiting for them to spring to life and continue the deadly battle against the invisible foe before them.

If Mead did not do them, he must have secured more talented sculptors for the four groups of figures. These are marvelous examples of a genius' labor of inspiration and insight. No breath of scandal touched these statutes. If Mead secured the talents of other artists, he acted more circumspectly in his later dealings with subcontractors. Just recently, they have been superbly refinished to their original condition.

A Springfield architect (formerly a carpenter), Thomas J. Dennis, revised the drawings for the Lincoln Monument and estimated the costs before sending the plans on to Richardson for execution. This contractor at last put the capstone atop the obelisk on September 19, 1871.

Dennis—about 47, a speculative mason, and one of the Directors of the National Lincoln Monument Association, and a native of Massachusetts—kept an office at the southeast corner of Sixth and Adams with Goyn R. Sutton under the firm name of Dennis & Sutton. Sutton came from New Jersey and was about 55 at this time. Both had previously been Mayors of Springfield—Sutton in 1860 and Dennis in 1865. In the Capital City, Sutton had designed Metropolitan Hall, and Dennis had served as the supervising architect of the Third Presbyterian Church.[82]

At this period of time, Knud Olsen and his wife, Bertha, resided in the Second Ward of Springfield on Mason between Taylor and Cox. Living with them were their sons George M., Charles J. and Otto, plus a daughter Emilia and evidently the maternal grandmother, called "Emma" Lund.[83] Olsen still earned his bread as a carpenter and reminisced many years later that the man he then worked for "had the blueprint for Lincoln's monument and he set a German man named [Christian] Wagner[84] and me to work making a model" of the Tomb.

Since Dennis redrew and reworked the building plans as an architect, he probably engaged Olsen and Wagner to fashion the necessary architectural model. Otherwise, their employer had to have been Richardson, the contractor. Such a scale model was vitally necessary, Olsen explained, to enable the stonecutters at the mines to cut and finish the rock correctly. Because Dennis & Sutton advertised as architects and builders, they probably had Olsen in their employ as a carpenter, anyhow.

As a man of eighty-two years, Olsen must have forgotten that he and Wagner actually fabricated two models. Dennis' drawings, we know, went to both Lemont, near Joliet, Illinois, where the interior and other stone was quarried, and to Quincy, Massachusetts, where the granite facing was mined and finished. Vermont also furnished marble for the project.[85] So, two models must have been prepared. Anyhow, two scale models of the Tomb still exist today. One of them is owned by the Illinois Funeral Directors Association in Springfield. The second, by the Canal Museum at Lockport, Illinois.

At some time after the fifteenth of August in 1870, Olsen moved his family to an eighty-acre farm he purchased in Section 20 of New Denmark Township of Brown County, south of Green Bay, Wisconsin.[86] Then, according to his own account, the Olsens went to Middle Inlet, Marinette County, Wisconsin, in 1879. When the Federal census taker visited Peshtigo Township in Marinette County in 1900, he found Bertha Olsen living with her son, Charles, and his family. But Knud was not included in this household. He, perhaps, was working on a building project, or back on the farm in New Denmark.[87] However, in 1905 when the State census taker made his enumeration of Stephenson Township in Marinette County, he reported that both Knud and Bertha

Olsen were residing with their son, Charles. Knud still gave his occupation as that of a carpenter.[88]

In October of 1911, Knud and Bertha Olsen migrated westward to Gridley, Butte County, California. There, Bertha died on November 17, 1912, and was buried in Live Oak Cemetery. Her husband seems to have gone back to Wisconsin after this time, but he returned to Gridley just a year and ten months prior to his death. Knud lived in the Golden State like a tough old Viking until Odin, the Keeper of Valhalla, welcomed him at 2 a.m. on August 21, 1921.[89] In just eighty-one days, Knud would have been 83 years of age. His life had been long and useful. At 82, Knud had declared that he enjoyed his "fishing trips as well as any man of today though I do get quite tired from a long walk in the heat and fighting mosquitoes."[90]

It would appear that the Lincolns kept their frame dwelling in reasonable repair, both for their own benefit and that of the several others who stayed with them from time to time. From census returns, we can prove that Mary Lincoln kept a servant whenever possible. In 1850, Catherine Gordon—and Irish lass of eighteen—resided with the Lincolns even before the house underwent expansion. Likewise, in 1855, a female between 10 and 20—but nameless in this state census—slept with the Lincoln household.

Sometime between 1856 and 1857, Stephen Smith (October 22, 1829—April 8, 1897), a brother of Mrs.

Lincoln's brother-in-law Clark Moulton Smith, rented a sleeping room with the Lincolns but took his meals elsewhere. Prior to this date, he had become a speculative mason (in Lodge No. 71) and followed the Methodist faith. He stayed with the Lincolns until he married. This rental to Smith proves that with the second story added in 1856, Mrs. Lincoln had space to spare.

By July 14, 1860, two domestic servants occupied quarters in the Lincoln residence. At that time, even more space existed at 8th and Jackson, because Robert Lincoln had gone to the East for schooling in August of 1859, leaving just Willie and Tad at home with the parents. Mary Lincoln had hired the services of a girl by the name of "M. Johnson," eighteen years of age and born in Illinois. I discovered this was Mary Johnson from a letter Mary Lincoln wrote to Hannah Shearer of Springfield, Illinois, on Oct. 2, 1859: "Mary, the same girl, I had last winter, is still with me, a very faithful servant, has become as submissive as possible." [in Turner & Turner, *Mary Todd Lincoln* (N.Y.: Alfred A. Knopf, 1972), 59.].

The U.S. Census 1850 Sangamon Co., Ill., p 266A, 11. 16-22, lists Mary Johnson as an 8-year-old female born in Illinois and that her father was Henry Johnson, 35, a farmer born in Vermont. Her mother, Joanna, 28, was born in Illinois. The U.S. Census 1860, Sangamon Co., Ill., p. 296, 1. 23 ff. confirms the information on the parents. However, Mary Johnson, 18, Female, born in Illinois is listed with her parents and with the Lincoln household in 1860. This was not an unusual practice. She married Wesley Knous on October 1, 1862.

The second roomer was Phillip Dinkel, a lad of about fifteen and born in Illinois. He perhaps helped the Hon. A. Lincoln, Presidential candidate, with the household chores. Mary tended to put on airs with her elevated position, although the Presidential race changed Abraham but little.

Young Phillip's mother—Barbara Dinkel—was a widow and resided at No. 54 on the south side of Edwards Street, between Eight and Ninth, and must have needed an additional income. She lived near enough for Mary to have learned of her misfortune and to have assisted her. Mrs. Lincoln possessed a large and kind heart.

Barbara Dinkel, in 1860, was approximately thirty-five years of age and claimed Würtemberg, Germany, as her native land. In addition to Phillip, she had two younger children at home with her: George, 13, born in Illinois; and Mary, 11, also of Illinois. Two elderly relatives resided with her, too. They stemmed from Würtemberg, the same as Barbara did.

Where Phillip Dinkel went after the Lincolns departed for Washington is unknown. We do know that he died in Springfield on October 25, 1865, with consumption, the same dangerous disease which had snuffed out the life of little Eddie Lincoln in 1850 and probably caused the demise of Willie Lincoln on February 20, 1862, and even

Tad Lincoln later. Phillip had been the eldest son of Mrs. Dinkel and worshiped at the First Baptist Church. This denomination Abe Lincoln had favored in his youth.

For additional information on these roomers, consult the author's articles in the *Lincoln Herald,* LXVIII, 135-140; 175-185; U.S. Census 1860, Springfield, Sangamon County, Illinois, p. 126, 11. 23-28; and the *Illinois Daily State Journal*, October 27, 1865, p. 2. c. 5.

The sitting room of the Lincoln's in Springfield, Illinois, as drawn by an artist for *Frank Leslie's Illustrated Newspaper*.

The front parlor of the Lincolns home as sketched by the special artist of *Frank Leslie's Illustrated Newspaper* in late 1860 or early 1861.

The artist's rendering of the back parlor of the Lincolns' residence as it appeared when A. Lincoln was President-elect.

References

70 Power, ed., *History of the Early Settlers*, 87.

71 C.S. Williams, comp., *Springfield Directory. . .For 1860-61* (Springfield: Johnson & Bradford, 1860), 49.

72 *Ibid*., 116; U.S. Census 1860, Springfield, Sangamon Co., Ill., p. 132, 11. 15-24. The census taker wrote Olsen's first name very poorly and misspelled his last, too. He called him "Olson," but this carpenter sometimes called himself "Olson."

In making his final copy, he even miscopied the age and put down 12 instead of 22, but there is no doubt but what it is "Canute Olson" in the household. He is plainly listed as an "Apprentice Carpenter" born in Norway. Olsen himself said he lived with the Armstrongs and even heard him discuss the Chicago Nominating Convention of 1860 which selected Lincoln as the Republican candidate for President. Armstrong had gone to this meeting. The city directory confirms Olsen's residence.

73 *Illinois Daily State Journal*, Dec. 24, 1877, p. 4, cc. 2 and 5; Burial Records, MS., Oak Ridge Cemetery, Springfield, Ill. Lincoln Club described in *Illinois Daily State Journal*, Jan. 14, 1860, p. 3, c. 2. When the Springfield Mechanic's Union was formed in 1839, John Armstrong acted as the first Secretary of this scholarly institution. Minute Book, 11, MS., Illinois State Historical Library.

74 "Reminiscences of Knud Olsen" in Marinette (Wis.) *Eagle-Star*, June 14, 1920, p. 2, cc. 3-4, courtesy of James L. Hansen, State Hist. Soc. of Wisconsin.

75 Copy of lease in James T. Hickey, "Own the house till it ruins me," *Jour. Ill. State Hist. Soc*., LXXIV, 280 (Winter, 1981).

76 Marriage Records, III, 366, MS., County Clerk's Office, Sangamon Co. Bldg., Springfield, Ill.

77 Williams, comp., *Springfield Directory. . .For 1860-61*, 122.

78 *Ibid.*, 105.

79 U.S. Census 1860, Galena, Jo Daviess Co., Ill., p. 101.

80 R.L. Dudley, *Springfield City Directory, For 1869-70* (Springfield: Daily State Register, 1869), 146: U.S. Census 1870, Springfield, Sangamon Co., Ill., p. 464, 11. 29-36; *Reports Made to the General Assembly of Illinois At Its Twenty-Seventh Session* (Springfield: Ill. Journal Printing Office, 1871), I, 1042-1047. For the Wabash line, Richardson worked as a clerk, general passenger agent and "attended to their tracks." Upon leaving the Wabash R.R., he laid the water pipes for the city of Springfield. Then he contracted for the brickwork on the Macoupin Co. Courthouse at Carlinville. Next, Illinois Female College at Jacksonville and the machine shop for the T.W. & W. R.R. at Springfield. He held membership in Springfield Lodge No. 4 and Springfield Chapter No. 1 of the Royal Arch Masons. In 1876, while at Springfield, he received the contract to erect a courthouse in Rockford for Winnebago County. On May 11, 1877, the dome collapsed while under construction, killing seven workmen and injuring twelve more. Of the latter, two later died from their injuries. At the coroner's inquest, the jury cited the cause of the disaster as the "neglect of Henry L. Gay, the architect of the said building." Richardson was allowed to finish the structure. By 1890, Richardson was living in Buenos Aires, Argentina, but by 1891 he had established his home in Chicago. He took a demit from Lodge No. 4 in Springfield on August 7, 1893, and was heard from no more. *The History of Winnebago County, Ill.* (Chicago: H.F. Kett & Co., 1877), 362-384; Lodge No. 4 reports, MSS., Grand Lodge of Illinois, A.F. & A.M., Springfield.

81 *Illinois State Journal*, Sept. 20, 1871, p. 2, cc. 1-3. The original specifications clearly show Sturgis as the architect and Mead the sculptor. Papers of the National Lincoln Monument Assoc., MSS., Illinois State Hist. Lib. *Illinois Daily State Journal*, Oct. 17, 1874, p. 1, c. 1.

82 Dudley, *Springfield City Directory, For 1869-70*, 65, 165; U.S.

Census 1860, Springfield, Sangamon Co., Ill., p. 579, 1. 17; U.S. Census 1870, Springfield, Sangamon Co., Ill., 446, 11. 17-24; *Illinois Daily Journal*, July 26, 1851, p. 2, c. 1, Mar. 22, 1855, p. 3, c. 1. Thomas J. Dennis was initiated, passed and raised in Springfield Lodge No. 4, A.F. & A.M., during 1852-53.

83 Dudley, *Springfield City Directory, For 1869-70*, 136; U.S. Census 1870, Springfield, Sangamon Co., Ill., p. 517, 11. 8-14. The census taker garbled this Norwegian's first name, calling him "Newton" this time.

84 Dudley, *Springfield City Directory, For 1869-70*, 172. This is the only man by the name of Wagner in Springfield who was a carpenter. He lived on the corner of Cook and College.

85 John Carroll Power, *Abraham Lincoln* (Chicago: H.W. Rokker, 1889), 233, 237, 244 and 257. Being the first Custodian of the Lincoln Tomb and an amateur historian, Power had an interest in and access to the records and made an accurate study of them while they were all available.

86 On this date, the Olsens were still in Springfield, Ill. Of their children, Geo. M. was 9; Chas. J. was 6; Orneila [Emilia] was 4; and Otto was 3. U.S. Census 1870, Springfield, Sangamon Co., Ill., p. 517, 11. 8-14.

87 U.S. Census 1900, Peshtigo Twp., Marinette Co., Wis., E.D. 121 Sheet 3, 11. 1-6. Courtesy of James L. Hansen, State Hist. Soc. of Wis.

88 Wisconsin State Census 1905, Stephenson Twp., Marinette Co., 659, 11. 20-27.

89 Butte County Death Records, Book 1905-1917, page 60 and Book D, page 200, kept in Butte Co., Calif. These records give the length of time the deceased had lived there prior to death.

90 Marinette (Wis.) *Eagle-Star*, June 14, 1920, p. 2, cc. 3-4. Bernice M. Bordeaux, R.R. 1, Wallace, Michigan, has supplied much important information on the Olsens.

LUCIAN TILTON

Lucian Tilton, the railroad king, drawn by Dr. Lloyd Ostendorf from an actual photograph reproduced in Clint Clay Tilton, *Lincoln's Last View of the Illinois Prairies*.

The Tiltons

As mentioned previously, Abraham Lincoln leased his historic Springfield residence to Lucian Tilton on February 8, 1861, for $350 per year. Again, President-elect Lincoln had rented to a railroader, thus demonstrating once more his close association with kingpins who ran the transportation lines in Illinois. Tilton had been elected President of the newly-reorganized Great Western Railroad in May of 1859.[91] This company succeeded the old Northern Cross Road.

At the time Tilton struck his bargain with Lincoln, he was forty-nine and hailed from or near Hampton Falls, New Hampshire, where he had been born in 1812. A wealthy man and the son of John Tilton, he owned $2,000 worth of real estate and possessed a personal estate valued at $25,000.

Because Tilton had come into Springfield without his family, he needed only public boarding and lodging. Therefore, in 1859, he took his meals at the American House, a prominent hostelry at the southeast corner of Sixth and Adams streets on the Public Square. And when the enumerator saw him on July 23, 1860, we learn for the first time where he had his sleeping room. He resided just north across the street from the American House at the three-story Converse Building located on the northeast corner of Sixth and Adams. With him were nine other occupants. Indeed, Tilton enjoyed distinguished company in this fine, new, brick structure where Amasa M. Converse, a wealthy merchant from Connecticut, operated a grocery store on the first floor. Evidently, Converse rented out the top two floors, using rooms 8 and 9 himself. Among those in the building with Tilton were A.M. Converse; Ozias Mather Hatch, the Secretary of State; John George Nicolay, formerly Hatch's chief clerk; and F.W. Bowen, Superintendent of the Great Western R.R.[92] But Nicolay had received a promotion. Since May of 1860, he had been working as A. Lincoln's private secretary.

But as soon as his family from the East decided to join him, Tilton needed a large, comfortable, convenient, and prestigious private dwelling which befitted his august position. His fellow roomer, Nicolay, would have known just the place, and it was available. Eagerly, Tilton procured the Lincoln residence. He retained his office at the Great Western Railroad Depot, just a few blocks away from his rented home. Very handy, indeed.

On the extreme right of this picture is the Converse Bldg. It stood on the East side of the Public Square, and there A.M. Converse ran a grocery ("Provision Store," as he called it). Lucian Tilton rented a room in it, probably on the third floor. Sec. of State O.M. Hatch and John G. Nicolay also lived here in 1860. A. Lincoln came to this brick structure often. His barber, Wm. Florville, had his shop in the Converse Bldg. on the Adams Street side, not visible. Photo from the Ill. State Hist. Lib.

Although an important historical figure, Tilton has not been studied previously in any detail. He somehow learned civil engineering and became associated with the growing railroad industry. The New Hampshire Legislature gave a charter to the Cheshire Railroad on December 17, 1844. In August of the following year, Lucian Tilton was chosen by the directors as one of the two engineers. When the grading and track work for the Cheshire line had been completed in the spring of 1848, Lucian Tilton—then chief engineer—received high praise and credit for his "fine roadbed and splendid bridges." To span Branch River at South Keene, New Hampshire, Tilton constructed one of the finest stone-arch bridges in the United States. He obtained Roxbury granite from the Thompson farm, about one half mile from the site of the bridge. With it he erected a single-span bridge running ninety feet long and standing sixty feet high. It still exists today in majestic splendor, a tribute to his engineering abilities. Upon the opening of the Cheshire Railroad on May 16, 1848, Tilton served as the first superintendent.

Lucian Tilton took to wife Lucretia Jane Wood at Keene, N.H., on December 19, 1850. Rev. George G. Ingersoll married them. The bride had been born in Keene on June 10, 1824, the daughter of John Vose and Lucretia (Perry) Wood. (Her father lived from 1796 until 1834, and her mother, from 1797 to 1875.) Mr. Tilton continued to build railroads in that region. In 1849 he served as a consulting engineer for the Ashuelot Railroad of New Hampshire. From 1850 until 1853, he acted as superintendent of the Fitchburg Railroad. On his resignation from this post, he traveled out to the Middle West where there existed a great need for his engineering and organizational skills. Exactly when he came to Springfield, Illinois, is unknown. But he had appeared on the scene by the spring of 1859.

This stone-arch railroad bridge at South Keene, NH, designed and built by Lucian Tilton, still stands over Branch River. It carried the tracks of the Cheshire Railroad. Photo by Mr. and Mrs. Clair E. Wyman.

In taking a tearful and rainy departure from his hometown on the eleventh of February in 1861, Lincoln boarded a Presidential Special at the Great Western Depot, located on the southwest corner of Tenth and Monroe. On the train to welcome him aboard stood the cordial and handsome Lucian Tilton, President of the railroad. He had taken complete charge of the operation and would ride with Lincoln over the track controlled by the Great Western. Tilton and his superintendent had carefully chosen Walter C. Whitney to be the conductor; Elias H. Fralick, the engineer; and Thomas Ross, the brakeman. To pull the special, Tilton and Bowen picked the Wiley, a Rogers locomotive which could easily do thirty miles per hour.[93] Lincoln's tenant would treat him royally on the first leg of his journey to the Capital.

"And the war came," as President Lincoln recounted in his Second Inaugural Address. All through that agonizing Civil War, Mrs. L. Tilton gave her time and energy to nurse the sick or injured soldiers at the nearby army camps. For these patriotic and gallant efforts, she received much grateful praise. She also helped with the activities of the U.S. Sanitary Commission. Countless soldiers from Camps Butler and Yates at Springfield visited her home to catch a glimpse of the hallowed shrine where the Lincolns had once lived. These humble men and officers she cordially invited inside so that each might experience the feeling of knowing, somewhat, the great and good Lincoln.

We know for certain that in 1865 L. Tilton dwelt in the Lincoln home at Eighth and Jackson with two females between the ages of 30 and 40; one female between 40 and 50; and another female between 50 and 60. Therefore, five persons occupied the rented residence at that particular time in history.[94] It seems logical to suppose that these inhabitants were: (1) Lucian Tilton; (2) Catherine P. Tilton, his sister; (3) an unnamed domestic servant living there; (4)

Lucretia Jane, his wife; and (5) Lucretia (Perry) Wood, his mother-in-law and a widow since 1834.

There are two excellent descriptions of the Lincoln homestead while the Tiltons occupied it. On September 25, 1861, Corporal Thomas Clingman from Company A of the 46th Infantry Regiment, Illinois Volunteers, at Camp Butler visited the Lincoln homestead on Eighth Street and reported that the dwelling was a "plain house of a light brown color with green window blinds." On January 4, 1865, a noted Eastern editor, Theodore Tilton (1835-1907), called at the old Lincoln home and discovered to his great surprise that the renters were also named Tilton. The residents received him with "great cordiality," and there Theodore stayed "the entire afternoon till dark." A "Miss Tilton" even plucked some flowers from the garden and presented them to him. The impressed visitor marveled that they "were yet in bloom."

The following day, Theodore Tilton briefly described the house in a letter to his wife. He saw it as "a plain, two-story, wooden building, painted brown,—looking like the residence of a man neither poor nor rich." It reminded him of New England houses, except that it was not painted white.[95] Well, it should have been in New England style, because the Eatons who constructed it came from New Hampshire. A correspondent for the *New York Herald* wrote on August 8, 1860, that Lincoln lived in a house which reminded him of Gen. George Washington's headquarters at Cambridge,

Massachusetts, then occupied by the noted Henry Wadsworth Longfellow. A punster might have added that the rightful occupant of the Lincoln home was also a long fellow.

All his adult life, Tilton had built railroads and earned an excellent salary as a designing or consulting engineer on many lines in both New England and the Midwest. At his death, he was termed "one of the most eminent engineers in the Northwest." During his Springfield years, he also served as President of the Illinois & Southern Iowa Railroad. By 1865, he had been consulting engineer and President of the Toledo, Wabash & Western as well as a director of that company. His various lines eventually became woven into the huge Wabash network. As a mark of esteem, the town of Tilton (near Danville, Illinois) was named for him.

Always interested in charity work, Mrs. L. Tilton gave of her time as one of the managers at the Springfield Home for the Friendless. She helped this institution just prior to her departure from Springfield. It had been established on Lincoln's birthday, February 12, 1863, to care for a passel of children who had been orphaned in Arkansas because of the Civil War. In 1865, its permanent building opened on South Grand Avenue, between Seventh and Eighth streets.

Lucian Tilton and his respected family remained in the Lincoln home until May 1, 1869, at which time they moved up to Chicago. This change of base had been contemplated by Lucian since January 2nd that year. When Robert Lincoln learned of Tilton's termination of the lease, he wrote: "I need not say how much I regret your intention." "The great courtesy exhibited by you and your family, towards strangers visiting this house, who must have given you so much trouble, will always be gratefully remembered," Robert promised.

In that railroad capital of the world, the Tiltons took occupancy of a house at 363 Ontario Street in the 20th Ward of Chicago. At this location the family finally got recorded in a census, name by name. For the first time, we can quote an official governmental source compiled by B.F. Butler and say for sure who lived with L. Tilton, railroad president. Listed with him was Lucretia Jane (Wood) Tilton, his wife, 46 years of age in 1870 and born in New Hampshire. Also in the household was Lucretia Perry Wood, 73 and a native of New Hampshire. This dowager was, of course, Lucian's mother-in-law. Living there, too, was Catherine P. Tilton, 45, from New Hampshire. She seem, to have been Lucian's sister and the one identified as "Miss Tilton" in 1865 down at Springfield. Two domestic servants did the housekeeping and cooking for the Tiltons. These live-in employees were Berletta Nicholas, 19, born in Illinois of foreign-born parents; and Emily Ellings, 29, from Norway.[96] In that same year, Lucian Tilton contributed to a fund collected to purchase a Lincoln bust by Leonard Wells Volk for display in the Chicago Historical Society. Tilton still held his old landlord in great esteem—or so it would appear from the records.

According to local traditions, the Tiltons' dwelling vanished into the torrid flames of the terrible Chicago Fire which destroyed that city on October 8, 1871. With their cherished abode went the priceless furniture which Lucian Tilton had purchased from the Lincolns in 1861.[97] Nevertheless, they did not lose their acquired fortune, and the Tiltons gradually resumed their position of leadership in the expanding and rebuilding community. Lucian became a director of the giant Illinois Central Railroad and sat on its board from 1871 to 1875. In the latter year, he won election as Vice President of the North Chicago City Railway Company. He kept his office at 71 Washington Street.

In the Tiltons' home, Lucian's mother-in-law, Lucretia (Perry) Wood, succumbed on August 25, 1875, at the age of 78. Her daughter and son-in-law shipped her body home to Keene, New Hampshire, for funeral services and burial in the family plot there.[98]

Lucian and Lucretia Jane eventually reëstablished a beautiful home at 297 Oak Street. And in that mansion Lucian Tilton died at the age of 65 on March 19, 1877, as a result of tuberculosis. Called "Colonel" by the press, he left a massive fortune of a quarter million dollars in cash and bonds; $60,000 of it in gold. He had drawn his will just the day before he succumbed.

The Rev. Dr. Robert Collyer, pastor of the Unity Church on North Dearborn Avenue at the southeast corner of Walton Place, gave the eulogy for Tilton on March 21st.

Since Collyer identified himself as a Unitarian minister, it can be assumed quite safely that this was the faith of the Tiltons, too. Dr. Collyer told his listeners that "Mr. Tilton was a courteous and energetic gentleman, who drew about him a wide circle of friends." "In his hospitality," Collyer declared, "he was bounteous, and his charity was proverbial." Sadly, though, the couple had no living children. A temporary burial took place in a vault at Graceland Cemetery, situated on the Green Bay Road, five miles north of the Courthouse. At some time in the future, a reporter learned, his body would be "taken East for final burial."[99] Mrs. Tilton had decided to inter her husband in her own family burial ground back at Keene, New Hampshire.

Widow Tilton set up her last home at 24 Junior Terrace where she continued her church and charitable work. In her home had been organized the Illinois Training School for Nurses. She had been a charter member of the Chicago Woman's Club and belonged to the Fortnightly Club. Then, in 1897, she joined the Chicago Historical Society as an annual member.

At 4:40 p.m. on November 4, 1906, after several weeks of illness, Mrs. Tilton passed away in her residence at the age of 82 plus. Her physician testified that she had suffered from an infection resulting from an abscess deep within one of her limbs. Actually, simple exhaustion caused her demise, he reported. Her body was quietly returned to Keene, New Hampshire, the place of her birth.[100] She had died on the wedding anniversary of the Lincolns.

There, two days later, her remains were deposited beside her husband's in Lot 43, Section 5, located in the old part of peaceful Woodland Cemetery at Keene. Her vital records were recorded on a large stone cross. Once more, they were together in the town where they had met and married so many years before. Mrs. Tilton's distinguished family also lay within this same ample lot. She had sprung from a lineage which included at least one general and a physician.

Lucian and his sister, Catherine P. Tilton (1824-1900), have separate-but-similar headstones positioned on either side of Mrs. Tilton's cross. Both are richly carved and ornamented. Lucian's has lifelike burr-oak leaves and acorns suitably draped in an attitude of mourning over the tops and sides. Catherine Tilton's is topped with flowers and ferns. Rarely is such fine sculpture seen on private tombstones.

As a motto, Lucretia had carved on Lucian's stone: "He that walketh uprightly, walketh surely." At the base of the Tilton family monument which marks Lucretia's grave, one sees these words: "Blessed are the dead who die in the Lord. . . ., that they may rest from their labors; and their works do follow them."[101] And their works have been followed and brought to light once more in this chapter, even though New Hampshire and Illinois are separated by hundreds of miles.

Lucian Tilton's tombstone in Woodland Cemetery at Keene, New Hampshire, is ornately carved with burr-oak leaves and acorns. Photo by Mr. and Mrs. Clair E. Wyman.

References

91 *Daily Illinois State Journal*, May 14, 1859, p. 3, c. 1. His first name in often spelled "Lucien." But to our knowledge, he had no middle name. He signed his name simply "Lucian Tilton" or "L. Tilton." There is no middle initial on his tombstone.

92 U.S. Census 1860, Springfield, Sangamon Co., Ill., p. 263, 1. 23; *Williams' Springfield Directory, 1860-61*, 136.

93 *Illinois State Journal*, Feb. 11, 1861, p. 2, c. 1; Chicago *Daily Tribune*, Feb. 11, 1861, p. 1, c. 3. Walter C. Whitney became a member of Springfield Lodge No. 333, A.F. & A.M. He also was exalted as a Companion in Springfield Chapter No. 1, Royal Arch Masons, during 1862-63. He served as Alderman in the 4th Ward at one time.

94 *Annual Report of the Chicago Historical Society 1906*, 95; Illinois State Census 1865, Springfield, Sangamon Co., p. 74, 1. 27, MS., Illinois State Archives; The *Chicago Daily Tribune*, Nov. 5, 1906, p. 5, c. 2.

95 Diary of Thomas Clingman, courtesy of Jim Bade of San Benito, Texas; Theodore Tilton to Elizabeth R. Tilton, Bloomington, Ill., Jan. 5, 1865, in Chicago *Daily Tribune*, Aug. 13, 1874, p. 2, c. 6.

96 *Holland's Springfield City Directory For 1868-9*, 37; Chicago Census Report. . .[1871] (Chicago: Richard Edwards, n.d.), 1106; U.S. Census 1870, Chicago, Cook Co., Ill., p. 459 B, 11. 27-32. The census was taken for this 20th Ward on July 23, 1870. Thanks to Patricia Ann Hauversburk for reading this census; there is no index.

97 A.L. Bowen, "A. Lincoln: His House," *Lincoln Centennial Association Papers* (Springfield: Lincoln Centennial Assoc., 1925), 48.

98 Clint Clay Tilton, *Lincoln's Last View of the Illinois Prairies* (Danville: Privately Printed, [1937]; *The Lakeside Annual Directory of*

the City of Chicago (Chicago: Donnelley, Loyd & Co., 1876-77), 998; Chicago *Tribune*, Aug. 27, 1875, p. 8, c. 7.

99 *The Lakeside Annual Directory of Chicago*, 39, 271, 1013; *The Chicago Daily Tribune*, Mar. 20, 1877, p. 8, c. 7, Mar. 22, 1877, p. 8, c. 4; Cook Co. death record,courtesy of Stanley T. Kusper, Jr.

100 *The Chicago Daily Tribune*, Nov. 5, 1906, p. 5, c. 2, p. 12, c. 1; Cook Co. death record, courtesy of Stanley T. Kusper, Jr.

101 Vital Statistics for Keene, N.H., Woodland Cemetery Records, and genealogical records researched by Mrs. Clair E. Wyman, West Swanzey, N.H.

Col. Geo. H. Harlow and his family occupied the Lincoln home from 1869-1877. Copy by Al Von Behren from an original print in the Illinois State Historical Library.

The Harlows

George Henry Harlow signed a formal lease and occupied the Lincoln home shortly after the Tiltons left in May of 1869. He paid the same amount of rent that Tilton had. Because Robert T. Lincoln did not live in Springfield, he relied upon his old boyhood chum, Clinton L. Conkling, to supervise the renting of the Lincoln property from then on. Conkling (born in Springfield October 16, 1843) had graduated from Yale and was now an attorney at Fifth and Monroe.

Robert Lincoln explained to Harlow on May 3 that he did not wish any changes "to be made in the house of anything like a permanent character such as closing up or opening doors or windows." Furthermore, Robert asked that "nothing [be] done to the property except what is essential." He did, nevertheless, authorize Harlow to whitewash the kitchen.

Harlow, at that time Illinois' Assistant Secretary of State, had been born September 5, 1830, in Sackets Harbor,

Jefferson Co., New York, the son of Daniel and Mercy (Austin) Harlow. At eighteen, he began to learn carpentry and joiner's work from Lewis Chambers of Deer River, New York. Upon reaching his twenty-first birthday, Harlow entered the office of O.L. Wheelock at Watertown, New York (later, Wheelock moved to Chicago), and studied designing, drafting and architecture.

Looking westward for an income, he went out to Pekin, Illinois, in March of 1854. "He soon found, however, that there was little demand for fancy architecture, and was compelled to lay aside his T square and pencil, and take up his jack plane and hammer." For $1.75 a day, he worked steadily for about fifteen months before becoming a clerk in a store operated by James Milner in Pekin. Other business ventures followed.

On October 1, 1856, Harlow married Susan M. Baily, the daughter of Samuel P. and Mary (Dorsey) Baily. The Hon. Sam Baily practiced law in Pekin, having come there from Pennsylvania by the way of St. Louis.

Formerly a Whig, Harlow joined the Republicans for the 1858 campaign and distributed that party's literature from his place of business. Next, he ran for Circuit Clerk in 1860 and won, being the only Republican elected in Tazewell County.

As soon as open hostilities flared between the North and the South, Harlow helped organize the Union League of America at the city of Pekin. Quickly this organization spread throughout the North. A state council for Illinois was organized on September 24, 1862, and soon its headquarters was established in Springfield. Being the Grand Secretary, Harlow moved down to the capital city in 1863. This important patriotic body fiercely supported the Northern cause and the Union Army.

At Springfield, Harlow advanced in the Republican Party. On January 2, 1865, he was elected First Assistant Secretary of the Senate. But on January 17, Governor Richard J. Oglesby selected Harlow as his private secretary. Following this post, he became Assistant Secretary of State in 1869.

During Harlow's tenancy of the "Railsplitter's" house, it had been given the street number of 430 South Eighth. For his listing in one city directory, Harlow put down that he resided in "Lincoln's old home." Being an Episcopalian, he attended St. Paul's Church at the southeast corner of Third and Adams where he officiated as a Vestryman and the Superintendent of the Sunday School.[102] He also joined St. Paul's Lodge No. 500, A.F.&A.M., where he assisted by filling several minor chairs even after he himself had become a Past Master.[103]

It seems obvious that Secretary Harlow had many personal and public responsibilities so that once in awhile he forgot to pay his rent to Robert Lincoln on time. And Robert—like his mother—always wanted his money on time. When such a lapse of memory occurred, Robert quickly reminded Harlow of this shortcoming and complained.

A Colonel on the Governor's staff immediately following the actual fighting of the Civil War, Harlow had served as Assistant Inspector General. In this post he supervised the mustering out of troops at Camp Butler, near Springfield. His high rank certainly made Harlow well aware of his importance in the community. As a result, he may have felt that he must posture somewhat for the public. While in the Lincoln home in 1870, Col. Harlow kept not one but two domestic servants in the house to help his wife. Both were white and thirty-three years of age. Eliza Rice had been born in Indiana, and Annie Adams came from Kentucky. Also living there with Harlow were his wife, Susan M., six years younger than himself; and four of their children: Richard Austin, 10; Bessie Baker, 8; Georgia Clarissa, 6; and Kate Louise, 3.[104]

Sadly, though, Kate, at the tender age of three years and ten months, succumbed in the Lincoln house on February 17, 1871. In the following month, Col. Harlow purchased Lot 55 S1/2 in Block 9 at Oak Ridge Cemetery and buried her small body there. (It had no doubt been held in the public receiving vault at Oak Ridge during this interim, as had Lincoln's.) Her death marked only the beginning of the sorrows which plagued the Harlows.

Secretary Harlow's parents were living with his sister, Mrs. J.M. Cramer of Fairbury, Livingston County, Illinois, when Mercy (Austin) Harlow died there on July 9, 1875. Harlow immediately sent for his mother's corpse and buried it at Springfield in his lot. His widower father, Daniel Harlow, immediately came to live with George and his wife in the renowned residence of the Lincolns at Springfield. (Daniel succumbed August 8, 1877, but by this time, the Harlows had moved to the corner of Fifth and Allen.) Next, Howard Bernard Harlow, the youngest son of Col. and Mrs. Harlow, passed away on October 19, 1877, after having suffered a week with scarlet fever. He was nearly four,[105] and of course had been born in the Lincoln home.

On January 13, 1873, Harlow had become the Secretary of State and held this elected position until January 17, 1881. He and the City of Springfield experienced a great honor in 1874. President and Mrs. Ulysses S. Grant steamed into town aboard a Presidential Special which arrived at 8 a.m. on October 14 over the tracks of the T.W.W. Railroad. They came for the dedication of the Lincoln Tomb. Gov. John L. Beveridge, a fellow Republican, met the First Family at the depot and escorted them to the Executive Mansion.

Secretary Harlow had greatly admired the Sixteenth President. He exhibited an oil portrait of Lincoln in his office at the State House. And for this special occasion, he tastefully decorated the sentimental old Lincoln home where he resided. Wreaths of evergreen, "festooned from point to point," hung on the historic house. In addition to flags, he put a portrait of Lincoln over the main entrance to the residence, suitably ornamented with red, white and blue. Under that, he placed a sign which said, "Welcome." "The gateway," reported the press, was "spanned with an arch of evergreens, and on the top of this [was] a stuffed eagle with wings wide spread, in the attitude of protecting a medallion representing Mr. Lincoln." Even the front fence displayed "evergreen wreaths festooned from point to point." Being a member of the Masonic Fraternity, Harlow had a deep reverence for the evergreen, or acacia, used in its rituals. Quite naturally he chose it to tell the world that Lincoln was indeed immortal.

On the morning of October 15, a slight rain fell, as if the heavens were weeping for the martyred Lincoln. When President Grant climbed into his special carriage that morning shortly before 10 a.m. under clearing skies, he immediately recognized the competent driver on the front seat. There, holding the reins tightly, sat James Smith who worked for Johnson & Co., operators of the Leland Stables. During the Vicksburg Campaign, Smith had acted as Grant's orderly. What a pleasant surprise the committee on arrangements had prepared for Pres. "Sam" Grant, one general who never forgot the loyal enlisted men who had served him so faithfully in the Civil War.

Promptly at 10 a.m. the parade formed on North Sixth Street under the direction of Gov. Beveridge, the Grand Marshall. Many units would help escort Pres. Grant, including the Springfield Commandery of Knights Templar and the band from the University of Illinois. Mrs. Grant rode in her own carriage with friends. South they went on Sixth to Adams, east on Adams at Eighth and south on Eighth past the Lincoln home so that the President might catch a glimpse of the abode where once had lived his old Commander-in-Chief. At Cook Street the procession turned west and finally ended up at the Lincoln Tomb where Grant presented the longest speech he had ever given as President of the United States. It was a brilliant effort and well received. Harlow rode with the other State officials in carriages. It was a proud day for him.[106]

Somehow, M.B. Church, a former law student in the firm of Lincoln & Herndon, learned that Secretary Harlow held a deep reverence for the memory of A. Lincoln. Therefore, on December 20, 1876, Church presented Harlow with one of the office chairs used by Lawyer Lincoln. An editor of the *Daily Illinois State Registor* witnessed the presentation and reported the ceremony in his paper that day on page four, column three.

After trying unsuccessfully to purchase the Lincoln home from Robert T. Lincoln for $2,000, Harlow finally rented another property in the spring of 1877. The Harlows transferred their abode to 1104 South Fifth.

One of the noteworthy events which occurred during Harlow's tenure as Secretary of State concerned the infant telephone, not even patented until March 7, 1876, by

Alexander Graham Bell of Boston. An astute, consummate, and shrewd politician, Secretary Harlow had telephones installed for the use of the 31st General Assembly (Jan. 8, 1879-May 31, 1879). Not even the White House in Washington, D.C., had a phone until President Grover Cleveland's occupancy (1885-89). At the end of the 31st G.A.'s session, Harlow ordered a telephone for the Executive Office of the Governor. Its use began May 31, 1879, as the legislators left town. Next, having carefully taken care of the egotisms of those who outranked him, Harlow rented an instrument for himself on March 19, 1880, from the Western Union Telegraph Co. which also operated the phone lines in Springfield.[107] Its first wires here had been installed on March 1, 1878.

After leaving office, Col. Harlow removed to Chicago and sold real estate. He died at his residence in Highland Park, Lake County (a suburb of Chicago) on May 16, 1900, as a result of asthma. His body was returned to Springfield and buried in Oak Ridge Cemetery.[108] Once again, he rested in the Lincoln legend.

After George Harlow's death, his wife, Susan M., went to live with her son, Richard A. Harlow, in New York. There, she died on January 25, 1916, and the son brought the body back to Springfield for burial in the family plot.

References

102 *Springfield City Directory. . .1877-78* (Springfield: M.G. Tousley & Co., Jan., 1877), 47; *Wiggins' City Directory, of Springfield, Illinois, For 1872-73* (Springfield: Ill. State Register, 1872), 52; *History of Tazewell County, Illinois* (Chicago: Chas. C. Chapman & Co., 1879), 707-709.

103 Records of St. Paul's 500, MSS., Grand Lodge A.F. & A.M. of Illinois, Springfield, Ill. Clinton L. Conkling was also a member of St. Paul's 500 but was not raised until June 9, 1881. By that time, Harlow was probably already in Chicago after leaving the Secretary of State's Office.

104 U.S. Census 1870, Springfield, Sangamon Co., Ill., p. 430 A, 11. 6-13.

105 *Springfield City Directory. . .1877-78*, 47; Death Records and newspaper obits.

106 *Illinois Daily State Journal*, Oct. 15, 1874, p. 1, cc. 5-6; Oct. 16, 1874, p. 2, cc. 2-4; Oct. 17, 1874, p. 4, c. 2.

107 Auditor's Receipts Nos. 4018, 4022, and 6096, MSS., Illinois State Archives.

108 *Chicago Daily Tribune*, May 18, 1900, p. 2, c. 5; Burial Records, MSS., Oak Ridge Cemetery, Springfield, Ill.

The Lincoln family kitchen in their home at Eighth and Jackson streets in Springfield, Illinois after they acquired a stove. The cookstove is the original used by the Lincolns and their hired help. Photo by Winfred "Doc" Helm

The Akards

On June 20, 1877, a man by the last name of Akard—Jacob D. Akard—took over the Lincoln home. At the time that he leased it, Jacob Akard was forty years of age. He had been married nearly eleven years to a woman named Letitia F. Gillman, thirty-seven, born in Illinois. They then had two living children, Mary Frances, about eight; and Edward, about four, who romped and played throughout the revered rooms of the Lincoln property. Jacob's father-in-law also shared the famous home with them. Stemming from New Hampshire, Ezra Gillman was a man 75 years of age, retired, and a widower. His wife had once run a boarding-house, a small, but important fact.

Jacob D. Akard had been born somewhere in Illinois on June 22, 1837, the son of Benjamin White and Margaret E. (Waggoner) Akard, Sr. Benjamin and Margaret were both natives of Tennessee. They had arrived in Illinois, the Prairie State, at least by 1837 because their oldest child, Jacob D., was born here in that year. We know for sure that they had put down roots in Madison County at least by the time the 1840 census was taken. Ten years later, Benjamin W. toiled as a bricklayer to support his rather large family at Upper Alton, Madison County, where he had by then acquired $3,000 worth of real estate. (The Akards had probably been in Upper Alton since their arrival in Illinois, but the 1840 census gives no exact locations within a county.) By 1850, they had six children: Jacob D., Mary E., Nancy, Margaret E., George H., and William.

Benjamin W. Akard had taken his family to Springfield by 1858 or '59. There, he found employment as a bricklayer and resided at the southwest corner of Madison and First. Often, he changed his residence as well as his livelihood. At the end of the Civil War, he listed himself as a cattle dealer, and by 1870, Benjamin had selected still another career. About that time, he took his departure from Springfield and became a sewing-machine salesman throughout Jersey County, approximately sixty miles southwest of Springfield. Among the popular makes being sold in the Springfield area were Howe, Singer and Victor. What company he represented we do not know.

Although single and of prime military age when the Civil War broke out, J.D. Akard did not volunteer for service. He remained at home where he was first noticed as a worker in his own right at Springfield about 1863. In that year he laid bricks with his father and resided with him on South Twelfth Street. As a boy, he had, without doubt, learned this building skill from Benjamin. Certainly he had labored beside his father prior to this date, but the directories took no notice of him. Whenever necessary, he could always fall back on this construction trade, an operative mason.

However, two years afterwards, Jacob managed the First Ward Meat Market on the corner of Seventh and Madison; naturally, he now proclaimed himself a butcher. He remained living on the southwest corner of Douglas and South Twelfth Street with his father. (His name is often spelled as "Ackard" or other corruptions.) Since his father then dealt in cattle, it seems quite logical that Jacob would try selling meat in a butcher shop.

Jacob D. Akard married Letitia F. Gillman (daughter of Ezra and Eliza Gillman) at Springfield on October 16, 1866. The Reverend Mr. Albert Hale, minister of the Second Presbyterian Church (now called Westminster), performed the nuptial ceremony. It should be assumed that Rev. Hale represented the religious denomination favored at least by Miss Gillman, if not by the groom, also.

During the year following his marriage, Jacob's meat market passed out of existence. J.D. Akard then announced that he was once more a mason by trade. Like father, like son, Jacob switched occupations frequently, jumping back and forth from one to another. Likewise, he changed his domicile, also. The young couple boarded now at the corner of Walnut and Washington streets.

When the Federal census taker, William P. Emery,

interviewed them on July 12, 1870, he learned that Letitia and Jacob Akard had a daughter, Mary Frances, who was then one year of age. The Akards slept in a household headed by Letitia's father, Ezra Gillman, 68. There was no Mrs. Gillman with them. Jacob still earned his family's bread as a brick mason. They shared the dwelling with George R. Pinckard, 27, a carpenter; his wife, Elizabeth J., 25; and their infant son, Frank, 3. Also with this clan lived two of Ezra Gillman's daughters: Laura E., 22; and Eveline E., 15.

As a man used to imitating his father, J.D. Akard became an agent for sewing machines shortly before 1872. He occupied housing on the south side of Market (now Capitol), near College. During 1873 and 1874, he seems to have been absent from Springfield. In fact, he may have been out selling with his father in Jerseyville and vicinity. When he returned with his family to Springfield, Jacob rented a place on Eighth Street between Allen and Scarritt. He published his occupation as sewing-machine agent. A year later—about 1876—he had his family under roof in a rented house at 429 West Market (the northeast corner of Lewis and Market), had five in his household, and still gleaned a precarious income as a "traveling agent" for sewing machines. He seems to have sold door to door in the Sangamon County area. His next choice of abodes was the Lincoln home which he leased in 1877.

Sometime after renting the A. Lincoln property, Akard undoubtedly turned it into a boardinghouse. Always greatly influenced by his relatives, Jacob Akard again had a close example to follow. His wife, Letitia, had grown up in a boardinghouse managed by her mother, Eliza Gillman, a New Hampshire native with no real estate to her name. Now, Letitia's father resided with them, and he may have reasoned, too, that the Akards could inaugurate a boardinghouse in this dwelling which had a built-in reputation and notoriety. This proposal seemed worth a gamble to Akard. From other evidence available, however, the property seems not to have been in very good repair. Thus, it possessed little attraction to reputable clients.

At least by 1878, the notable home of Lincoln had definitely become a tawdry boardinghouse, complained John Carroll Power, and Robert Lincoln did not deny or dispute this carping charge. (Power, a Custodian of the Lincoln Tomb, had won a local reputation as an author of books.)

As usual, Robert Lincoln experienced a few minor problems with Akard. For instance, he did not want to clean out the privy vault. Furthermore, with several families or individual occupants in the home, the water bill doubled, costing Robert more money for the utilities. This fact alone would indicate that the property had become a boardinghouse with many tenants. It is quite possible, though, that Akard and his family did not actually live on the premises for any great length of time.

In a city directory published in 1879—but most certainly compiled late in 1878, there is only this listing: "Lincoln's

Old Homestead, ne cor. 8th and Jackson." And a check of the entire directory does not reveal any person who was willing to give his or her address as the Lincoln house. In this same directory, J.D. Akard is set down as a butcher who resided on the east side of Eighth Street, between Edwards and Cook. This location is over a block south of the Lincoln home but on the same side of Eighth. Thus, he had already deserted the Lincoln home as his residence, or so it would appear.

Akard's lease from Robert Lincoln formally expired in June of 1879, but the directory cited above indicates that Akard had left long before the expiration of his contract. His boardinghouse venture had passed quickly into history. Actually, Robert did not even know that Akard had either moved out, or moved his tenants out, until his aunt, Ann Maria (Todd) Smith, informed him of this fact. According to a local publication, there was a period of time when the Lincoln home stood "empty and deserted and became headquarters for tramps and thieves." If this statement is true, it must have been during the period when Akard held the lease or immediately afterward.

Jacob and Letitia lost their ten-year-old daughter, Mary Frances, on October 25, 1879. She had occupied the Lincoln home for a short while with her parents.

In 1880, Jacob D. Akard still butchered for a living but by now had moved once more, this time to 1110 South Fourth. There, he lived with his family, plus Ezra Gillman, his seventy-eight-year-old father-in-law who had made his home with them for many, many years. (He was not even listed with his wife, Eliza, in the 1860 census.)

Although the Akards' address did not change the following year, the husband's occupation did. Again, he listed himself as a "machine agent," meaning sewing machine salesman. By 1883 or '84, Akard had rented a dwelling at 620 West Capitol Avenue. For his job classification, he simply said, "Agent."

On about January 1, 1885, the *Illinois State Journal* had learned "that Mr. Jacob Akard is dangerously sick." The editor reported this distressing information under his column titled "Local Brevities." But his announcement did not come out until the morning of January 2nd. On that very day Jacob died at the age of 47 1/2. However, both local papers failed to print an obituary of him or even mention that he had passed away. Perhaps for this reason, he has been an unsung figure in the Lincoln story, and no previous author has written his brief biography. Indeed, Akard's life has been extremely difficult for this author to trace.

Thomas C. Smith's funeral establishment at 325 South Fifth took charge of the body. They placed it in a chestnut casket, covered with black cloth, nicely trimmed and lined. It bore an engraved nameplate upon it, too. That coffin cost the family $55. The undertakers supplied crepe for mourning insignia at a cost of fifty cents. For $4.50 they opened a grave at Oak Ridge Cemetery in Lot 27, Block 12, which the father, Benjamin W. Akard, already owned. (He had purchased it

September 30, 1868.) Smith furnished a hearse and attendant, for eight dollars, and rented four carriages to the family at a price of $16. In all, the funeral expenses came to $84.

With sorrow and tears, family and friends paid their last respects to Jacob D. Akard on January 4. His burial site and monument stand high on a knoll just north of the Lincoln Tomb, and Jacob lies surrounded by other members of his family. For immediate neighbors, he has John Henry Schuck, who worked upon the Lincoln home as a skilled cabinetmaker/carpenter, and Governor William H. Bissell (1811-1860). Bissell sat as the first Republican Governor of Illinois, and A. Lincoln acted as his chief political advisor. Even in death, Jacob D. Akard occupies an eternal place in Lincoln historiography.

Jacob's father, Benjamin W. Akard, Sr., outlived him. The latter did not die until December 20, 1886, at the age of 73 years, four months and twenty days. He had been one of the first sewing machine agents in Jersey County and made his home in Jerseyville, the county seat. Well respected by his fellow citizens, Benjamin enjoyed "a large trade, but of late years [had] not been in active business." Two days following his death, Benjamin Akard's remains were returned to Springfield where they were placed in the lot which he owned at Oak Ridge Cemetery.

B.W. Akard's widow, Margaret E. (Waggoner) Akard, lived on in Jerseyville until she met death, also. She died at the home of her son, Benjamin W., Jr., a grocer, on March

23, 1908, at the venerable age of 91 years, 7 months and 20 days. Likewise, her body was shipped to Oak Ridge Cemetery for burial with her family. Thus passed the matriarch of the Akard household.

Jacob D. Akard's widow, Letitia F., shifted her home to Peoria within two years after her husband died. In that large city on the Illinois River she supported herself and her sons with her sewing machine and needle. She found rooms at 1425 Main Street and advertised as a "taloress." Afterall, her husband and father-in-law had demonstrated sewing machines. About a year later, however, she obtained a more secure position as Matron at the Home of the Friendless. Her pay in this office permitted her to afford schooling for her son, Edgar V. He later went to work for the F.F. Ide Manufacturing Company as a "wheel truer." Sadly, though, her youngest boy, Jesse, died at Peoria on June 10, 1895. Two days later, his remains joined those of his father in Springfield.

Letitia F. Akard remained in Peoria until shortly before the turn of the century. Where she lived immediately after this time, is not known. We do know, though, that she became an invalid and lived with her son or sons. During the summer of 1911, she went to Huntington, Indiana, and received shelter in the home of her only surviving boy, Edward, who had a residence at 207 Taylor Street. He held the position of Foreman in the Heel and Counter Department of the Barker-Brown Shoe Factory. There, in

Edward's house, Letitia Akard died on Sunday morning, January 25, 1914, at the age of 74. Funeral services took place at Edward's place on Monday evening at 7:30 under the direction of the Rev. William F. Smith, pastor of the First Methodist Episcopal Church. At 4:50 on Tuesday morning, her body was place aboard the Wabash train and returned to Springfield, Illinois, for burial that same day in Oak Ridge Cemetery beside her husband.[109] Edward Akard had also lived briefly in the Lincoln home with his parents.

Until James T. Hickey, of the Illinois State Historical Library, discovered Akard mentioned in the papers of Robert T. Lincoln, no scholar had ever heard of this family. Now, at last, Jacob and Letitia Akard have been restored to their rightful place in the tale of the Lincoln homestead.[110]

References

109 He is the only Akard in town during 1876. *Springfield City Directory. . .1877-78*, 8; U.S. Census 1860, Springfield, Sangamon Co., Ill., p. 345, 11. 1-12; U.S. Census 1850, Upper Alton, Madison Co., Ill., p. 397 A, 11. 41-43, 397 B, 11. 1-6; U.S. Census 1840, Madison Co., Ill., p. 143, 1. 4; *Buck & Kriegh's City Directory for the Year 1859* (Springfield: B.A. Richards & Co., 1859), 25; *Springfield City Directory. . .For 1864* (Springfield: Johnson & Bradford, 1864), 91; *Springfield City Directory. . .For 1866* (Springfield: Bronson & Nixon, 1865), 39, 41, 188; Marriage Records, IV, 223, MSS., County Clerk's Office, Sangamon Co. Bldg., Springfield; *Holland's Springfield City Directory for 1868-9* (Chicago:

Western Pub. Co., 1868), 50; U.S. Census 1870, Springfield, Sangamon Co., Ill., p. 199, 11. 38-40, p. 200, 11. 1-6; *Wiggins' City Directory, of Springfield, Illinois For 1872-73* (Springfield: Ill. State Register, 1872), 18, the printer listed his middle initial as "K.": *Babeuf's Directory of Springfield, Illinois. . .For 1875* (Springfield: Ill. Journal Co., 1875), 27; *Centennial. . .Directory of Springfield, Illinois* (Springfield: Ill. Journal Co., 1876), 48; *A Directory of the City of Springfield. . .For 1879-80* (Springfield: Ill. Journal Co., 1879), 105, 14; *Springfield in 1892: Souvenir Supplement Illinois State Journal*, 8; U.S. Census 1880, Springfield, Sangamon Co., Ill., E.D. 230, p. 35, 11. 27-30; *Gould's Springfield Directory, For 1880-81* (Springfield: David B. Gould, [1880]), 18; *J. Babeuf's Directory of Springfield, Illinois. . .For 1881-82* (Springfield: J. Babeuf, 1881), 18; *Babeuf's Directory of the City of Springfield. . .1884-5* (Springfield: J. Babeuf, 1884), 24; *Illinois State Journal*, Jan. 2, 1885, p. 8, c. 1; Jacob D. Akard's date of death is given within a section titled "In Memoriam" in *Babeuf's Directory of the City of Springfield. . .1886-7* (Springfield: J. Babeuf, 1886), 22; Jacob's date of death is confirmed by the inscription on his tombstone in Oak Ridge Cemetery and the burial records of Thos. C. Smith, Day Book, VI, 83, MSS., Boardman-Smith Funeral Chapel, Springfield, Ill.; B.W. Akard's Lot Record, MS., Oak Ridge Cemetery, 1441 Monument Ave., Springfield, Ill.; *Jersey County Democrat*, Dec. 23, 1886, p. 5, c. 5; *ibid*, Mar. 26, 1908, p. 11, c. 5; *Gould's Peoria City Directory For 1888-89* (Peoria: David B. Gould, n.d.), 104 and later directories; *Illinois State Journal*, June 12, 1895, p. 5, c. 6; *Huntington* (Ind.) *Herald*, Jan. 26, 1914, p. 8, c. 2, thanks to Mrs. Joan Keefer, Huntington Public Library: *Illinois State Journal*, Jan. 27, 1914, p. 10, c. 1. The Akards' son, Edgar V., evidently died before his mother. Yet, he is not buried in the family plot in Oak Ridge.

John C. Power, mentioned in this section, was admitted to St. Paul's 500, A.F. & A.M., on July 10, 1877, from Hartford Lodge 151, Hartford, Ind.

110 Hickey, "Own the house till it ruins me," *Jour. Ill. State Hist. Soc.*, LXXIV, 284-287 (Winter, 1981). Thos. C. Smith, the undertaker, held membership in Springfield Lodge No. 333.

QUIT-CLAIM DEED—Long Form.

This Indenture, Made this eighteenth day of April in the year of our Lord One Thousand Eight Hundred and Seventy-four BETWEEN Mary Lincoln, widow of Abraham Lincoln, deceased, of the City of Chicago in the County of Cook and State of Illinois party of the first part, and Robert T. Lincoln of the City of Chicago in the County of Cook and State of Illinois party of the second part

Witnesseth, That the said party of the first part, for and in consideration of the sum of Five Hundred Dollars, in hand paid by the said party of the second part, the receipt whereof is hereby acknowledged, and the said party of the second part forever released and discharged therefrom, ha[illegible] remised, released, sold, conveyed, and quit-claimed, and by these Presents do[illegible] remise, release, sell, convey, and Quit-Claim, unto the said party of the second part, his heirs, and assigns, FOREVER, all the right, title, interest, claim, and demand, which said party of the first part ha[illegible] in and to the following described lots, pieces, or parcels of land, situated in the County of Sangamon and State of Illinois and known and described as follows, to wit: The Lot number Eight (8) and the South ten (10) feet of Lot number Seven (7), all in Block number Ten (10) in E. Iles' Addition in the City of Springfield in the County and State last aforesaid

To Have and to Hold the Same, together with all and singular the appurtenances and privileges thereunto belonging, or in any wise thereunto appertaining; and all the estate, right, title, interest, and claim whatever, of the said party of the first part, either in law or equity, to the only proper use, benefit and behoof of the said party of the second part, his heirs, and assigns, forever.

And the said party of the first part hereby expressly waives and releases any and all right, benefit, privilege, advantage, and exemption, under or by virtue of any and all Statutes of the State of Illinois, providing for the exemption of homesteads from sale on execution or otherwise.

In Witness Whereof, the said party of the first part has hereunto set her hand and seal the day and year first above written.

Signed, Sealed, and Delivered, in the Presence of

Mary Lincoln [Seal.]

[Seal.]

[Seal.]

[Seal.]

State of Illinois
COUNTY OF Cook, City of Chicago } ss.

I, David B. Lyman a Notary Public in and for the said City and County, in the State aforesaid, Do hereby Certify, that Mary Lincoln who is personally known to me to be the same person whose name is subscribed to the foregoing Instrument, appeared before me this day in person, and acknowledged that she signed, sealed, and delivered the said Instrument as her free and voluntary act, for the uses and purposes therein set forth, including the release and waiver of the right of homestead.

Given under my hand and Notarial Seal this 18th day of April A.D. 1874.

David B. Lyman
Notary Public.

For $500, Robert T. Lincoln purchased his mother's share of the Lincoln home on April 16, 1874. The quit-claim deed was never recorded.

Copy courtesy of the late Ralph G. Newman

The Wendlandts

Gradually, the Lincoln homestead fell into disrepair through normal use as well as the absent owner's neglect. Lucian Tilton had spent $24.10 to repair the faulty roof in 1861 and 1862. Col. Harlow later discovered in 1871 that the old roof still leaked. He also informed Robert Lincoln that the timbers were decaying and the home needed a "thorough overhauling." Fix the roof, Lincoln told Harlow, but he neglected to say anything further. By 1873, Harlow estimated that the place needed $500 worth of reconstruction.[111]

Akard had slipped away from the property unnoticed and evidently left it in poor condition. Robert Lincoln finally determined to get out from under the constant upkeep of the home. He therefore asked the Lincoln Monument Association if it would accept A. Lincoln's Springfield house. This group met on July 31, 1879, and heard Robert's letter read. In it he admitted that "he or the family were not able to care for the property as it should be, but were willing to convey it to the Association in trust. . . ." Robert wished for the historic building to be kept open for sightseers.

At this special meeting, C.L. Conkling, the agent of Mr. Lincoln, stood and informed the body that "it was impossible to secure a tenant for the house in its present condition, and that it was necessary that some action be taken." After due deliberation, members of the Association decided that they had their hands full with the Lincoln Tomb and that the house did not fall within the province of their charter. For these reasons, they voted not to accept the proffered gift.[112]

When Robert Lincoln learned of this negative decision, he wrote on August 25, 1879, that he would have to make repairs on the house and "pay for them if I can. . . ." Already a potential tenant had inquired about renting it.

Thomas F. Nicholl desired to take over the vacant residence. He was about 55 years of age, born in England, and a civil engineer. He then lived at 516 South Sixth in a rented house with his wife, Ellen M., 52; and their children, Julia, 23; Lizzie, 21; Grace, 19; Fannie, 17; and Harry, 12, all born in Canada.[113] He moved about frequently in following his railroad profession, and Robert decided against him. He made a wise choice; within a year or so, Nicholl left Springfield.

Since he could not lease the house because of its rundown condition, Robert had some restorations done in 1879. Defective shingles covering the roof on the front portion of the house were replaced, we know.[114] Conkling probably saw to it that the place received a good cleaning and a little yard works, too. He must have spruced it up a bit with paint where needed.

Robert Lincoln explained candidly to Conkling, "As I cannot afford the expense of a private custodian, it will be best to rent the house. . .as soon as you can." By late 1879, Lawyer Conkling had found a reliable tenant for the Lincoln property. This time he rented to one of the most interesting and learned men in Springfield but until now a phantom figure completely forgotten. His name? Dr. Gustav Adolph Hermann Wendlandt, a licensed physician with flawless credentials. A native of Germany, he was a staunch Democrat and a Lutheran. Being a trained European scholar, he could translate German, Polish, French, Bohemian and Russian into English. Often the Illinois State Board of Health (created May 27, 1877) called upon Dr. Wendlandt for his linguistic skills and his formal knowledge of medicine. At the time he secured the Lincoln home, Wendlandt was past 36 years of age and about to be married.

Gustav A.H. Wendlandt, as he sometimes signed his name, was born in Prussia on May 27, 1843, the son of Michael and Caroline (Hennig) Wendlandt. His father taught school, and Gustav naturally received an excellent education in the traditional and stern manner then existing in the Kingdom of Prussia. In 1867, at the age of twenty-four, Gustav emigrated to the United States and settled at St. Louis, a thriving city with a large German population.

There, he established himself as a teacher in Carondelet, at that time a suburb southwest of St. Louis. He taught in a private school located at Second and Taylor.[115]

A serious throat disorder began to threaten his health, and this ailment forced him to leave the teaching profession. So, in 1871, Wendlandt entered Missouri Medical College in St. Louis (now Washington University School of Medicine). He chose as his preceptor Dr. Adam Hammer (1818-1878) whose specialities were surgery and pathology. Born in the Duchy of Baden in Germany, Hammer attended the renowned college of Heidelberg where he earned his M.D. degree in 1842. When the political revolutions of 1848 failed, Dr. Hammer escaped to America, reaching St. Louis October 28, 1848. Such action indicates that Dr. Hammer had supported the liberal cause and fought against the established government. Truly a scholar, he founded several medical schools. Then, on August 14, 1869, he joined the faculty of Missouri Medical College as Professor of Clinical and Operative Surgery and Pathological Anatomy. At Heidelberg, Hammer had studied in the Literary Department before turning to medicine.[116] Thus, he probably encouraged Wendlandt to write, also.

Midway in Wendlandt's studies, Prof. Hammer departed in a huff from Missouri Medical College rather than share responsibilities in surgery with a Prof. A.P. Lankford. Hammer quit on March 22, 1872, after a highly-publicized and raucous feud with Dr. Lankford and went back to private practice.[117]

Undaunted by the loss of his major professor, Wendlandt continued his courses and acquired the degree Doctor of Medicine on March 4, 1873. He graduated with honors, too. By "public competitive examination" in all branches of medicine taught there, Wendlandt won second prize: a case of surgical instruments. In chemistry, he shared second prize which consisted of books. The thesis which he submitted for graduation explained the "Circulation of Blood."[118]

After practicing about a year in St. Louis, Dr. Wendlandt departed in 1874 for Springfield, Illinois. He promptly leased space over 523 East Monroe Street where a fellow countryman, Henry Schlange, ran a cigar store. Being single and thrifty, Wendlandt probably slept in a room adjoining his office space. But he took his meals at the Jefferson House on the southeast corner of 7th and Washington.[119] Always scurrying about town in a rapid hurried manner, Springfieldians aptly nicknamed him "The Flying Dutchman."[120]

Wendlandt's path would often cross that of his neighbors downstairs. Henry Schlange, about two years younger than he, had been born in Germany, also. Although a tobacconist then, his occupation would change several times in the years to come. Schlange tried his hand at the grocery business and then by 1880 became the editor and publisher of a weekly German-language newspaper called the *Staats Wochenblatt*. Its office number was 514 East Monroe.[121] Dr. Wendlandt seems to have limited his associations to the German element of the city. One does not find him listed in other groups.

On May 29, 1877, Gov. Shelby Moore Cullom approved "An Act to regulate the practice of medicine in the State of Illinois." This legislation went into force July 1 that year and provided that every person practicing medicine in the State had to show his Doctor of Medicine diploma and be issued a certificate if he wished to continue in this profession. Non-degree physicians had to pass an examination to qualify.

Dr. Wendlandt presented his college credentials and stated that he had been engaged in medicine for six years. To arrive at this figure, he counted his full two years of medical schooling at Missouri Medical College. The State Board of Health certified him on October 20, 1877, and gave him registry No. 1413 on November 5. He listed his specialty as pathology.[122] Yet we know that he practiced surgery in addition to general medicine.

His reputation grew rapidly and spread widely. "Having been called several times from Springfield, Ill. to Milwaukee to patients living there," Dr. Wendlandt made many friends in Wisconsin. In some way he met Hedwig Hermine Richter, daughter of August Maximilian (1822-1907) and Christiane Friederike (Richter) (1828-1917) Richter of Manitowoc, Wis. Her parents were third cousins. This young lady had been born on December 9, 1857. In the hometown of the bride—on Lake Michigan about seventy-five miles north of Milwaukee—they were married December 30, 1879, by Michael Kirwan, the County Judge.

(Gustav was not so religious as to demand a church wedding though his second wife later described him as a "devoted" Lutheran.) C.F. Viebahn and Hugo Klingholz stood up with Gustav and Hedwig.[123]

After this short civil ceremony in the bride's home, Dr. Wendlandt escorted his young wife back to Springfield, Illinois. He had no doubt already engaged the Lincoln home prior to his marriage, since the 1880 directory shows him there. City directories are nearly always compiled in the year prior to the publication date. So, Wendlandt must have occupied it in the fall of 1879 as soon as adequate repairs had been made.

Dr. & Mrs. Wendlandt started housekeeping at 430 South Eighth Street, as the Lincoln home was numbered. The new bridegroom also opened his office there, moving it from a spot above 523 East Monroe.[124] A census taker called at the Wendlandts' residence on June 4, 1880, and reported that the wife had anglicized her first name from Hedwig to "Hattie." She told the questioner that she had been born in Wisconsin but that both her parents came from Saxony. Her age? Twenty-two. Her husband was thirty-seven. Living with them at this particular time was Max Rosner, a white male, forty-one years of age, single and with no occupation. He had been born in Germany.[125] Nothing further is known about him.

When the *Springfield Directory for 1881-2* appeared, it carried Dr. Wendlandt's name and address with an added identification: "Lincoln's old home."[126] That was a mark of distinction, even for a Democrat. And while the Wendlandts occupied the property, one of the two living Lincolns passed away. At 8:15 p.m. on Sunday, July 16, 1882, Mrs. Abraham Lincoln breathed her last at the home of Mr. and Mrs. Ninian W. Edwards on Second Street, the second house north of Edwards Street, in Springfield. In this very house of her sister and brother-in-law, she had been married nearly forty years previous to her demise. Thomas "Tad" Lincoln had preceded her in death, dying on July 15, 1871, in Chicago. Three years later, on April 16, 1874, Mary had sold her interest in her home to eldest son Robert for $500. Robert Lincoln alone possessed the old home at Eighth and Jackson.

After approximately three years in their prestigious location, Dr. & Mrs. Wendlandt forsook the capital city of Springfield. They moved down to Hoyleton, Washington County, Illinois, about fifty-five miles slightly southeast of St. Louis. But three years in that tiny town evidently proved to be quite sufficient.

Wendlandt and his helpmate must have enjoyed their previous sojourn in Springfield; for, about 1886, they went back there. This time they rented a house slightly out of the city limits at 1317 North Third Street. Dr. Wendlandt then set up his practice at 528 East Adams, located over 526, on the south side of the Public Square. Seeberger & Bro. (Lafayette and Meyer) operated a clothing store below him on the ground floor.[127]

Unfortunately, Mrs. Wendlandt's health began to decline rapidly. She seems to have suffered from consumption. Gustav determined to master this malady and arranged to study medicine at the University of Berlin. Hedwig went to live with her parents in Manitowoc, and the good Doctor departed for Germany. He found living quarters with a friend and enrolled for the winter semester of 1890-91. Every day he labored in the hospitals under the tutelage of the noted Dr. Robert Koch and other outstanding surgeons. Dr. Koch had been experimenting with a cure for consumption, and he presented three vials of his formula to Dr. Wendlandt.

Upon hearing that his wife was near death, Gustav cut short his schooling and came back to the United States about the first of February, 1891. He immediately hurried to Manitowoc with his "cure," but his beloved Hedwig died on February 8. With a broken heart, he interred her in the Richter lot of Evergreen Cemetery at Manitowoc, Wisconsin. There, she lies today with her parents and family.[128]

As soon as the pain had somewhat subsided, Dr. Wendlandt retraced his steps to Springfield. Now, he had even greater honors, having done postgraduate work at the University of Berlin. His old patients once more called, and he busied himself with medicine and politics at his same office which lay just to the south of the Old State House which Lincoln had made famous by his very presence there on numerous occasions. It then served as the courthouse for Sangamon County.

A forceful stump speaker despite his throat troubles and in great demand by his party, Dr. Wendlandt again supported Grover Cleveland for President. And when elected, Cleveland appointed Wendlandt a United States Surgeon to examine veterans of the Civil War for pensions or medical treatment.[129] In addition to personal speaking engagements, it would seem that he also supported the Democrats with his gifted and fluent pen. In time for the 1892 election, he established a German-language newspaper called *The Springfield Zeitung* which he edited and published himself at his office—by now renumbered to 526 1/2 East Adams from 528. The 1/2 acted as a new indication to show it was located above 526. Of course, medicine still earned his living.[130]

Having met Martha Butzow and fallen in love with her, Dr. Wendlandt married her in Chicago, Illinois, on April 3, 1893. The Rev. Louis Hoelter, pastor of the German Emanuel Evangelical Lutheran Church at 12th and Ashland Avenue, performed the ceremony. Martha had been born in the "Windy City" on January 31, 1865. Both her parents stemmed from Germany; thus, the Wendlandts had a common bond in their cultural backgrounds. She had counted just twenty-eight summers, while her professional and scholarly husband had seen nearly fifty. At the time of her marriage, Martha resided in Chicago,[131] but she now went to live in Springfield with her husband.

The happy physician continued to edit his little newspaper as well as minister to his trusting patients and adjust to the changing times. When the telephone became generally available, Dr. Wendlandt had one put into both his office and home.[132] Nevertheless, about 1897, he gave up his downtown office and saw clients only at his residence.[133] This move certainly saved a considerable amount of rent money that could be invested in his vanity publication which probably did not even earn its keep.

Dr. Wendlandt, for some unknown reason, determined to leave Springfield once more. On October 11, 1899, he purchased a house at 213 Short Street in Princeton, Green Lake County, Wisconsin. Not having the total price in hand, he mortgaged it. Six days later, he left Illinois, never to return.

Not until April 5, 1900, did Dr. Wendlandt apply for a license to practice medicine and surgery in Wisconsin. On his application, he stated that his "School of Practice" was Allopathy, probably meaning that he took advantage of all measures which would aid him in treating disease or illness. In answer to one question concerning advertising, Wendlandt reported that he had never advertised for patients and did not intend to do so at this late date. "My work," he boasted, "shall be the advertisement as it has been." On a line intended for "References as to Character," instead of listing names of persons, he wrote: "Setting aside modesty, I can rightfully say, my character is blameless." When requested to name his preceptor and give his current address, the good Doctor further exhibited his keen sense of biting humor by writing: "Prof. A. Hammer, St. Louis." "Now already long deceased," explained Wendlandt with irony, "his post office address therefore not known." Two physicians, S.R. Holly and N.G. McConnell, vouched for him, and the Wisconsin Board of Medical Examiners issued Wendlandt a license numbered 1185.[134] Afterall, he held an earned degree and had practiced with great skill for twenty-seven years.

Wendlandt found a great local need for his professional services since Princeton, a small village, did not even have "the required number of lawfully entitled physicians" to sign his application for a license. Citizens in that quiet little town discovered him to be "a good scholar and a great reader." Soon, he gathered about himself "a large circle of friends." They liked him because he "was a kind-hearted genial gentleman." Three years after settling there, Gustav started editing a German newspaper, the *Princeton Zeutybg*—just as he had done back in Springfield, Illinois. Black printer's ink mingled congenially with the red German blood in his veins.

After six months of serious illness, Dr. Wendlandt died in his home at 7 a.m. on October 16, 1909—the centennial year of Abraham Lincoln's birth. Cancer of the throat finally killed him despite his unflagging courage and his excellent medical treatment of himself for many years. His wife, as well as a brother and sister, survived him, the latter two residing in Germany. The Rev. Adolph G. Hoyer of St. John's Lutheran Church conducted the funeral two days later with burial being made in Princeton City Cemetery. Over his grave his loving widow erected a large impressive stone cross. On it a stonecutter incised Wendlandt's name and vital statistics in German.[135]

Martha Wendlandt then married Frank J. Yahr in May of 1911. A pioneer lumberman of Princeton, he had been born near Watertown on September 26, 1856. His first wife, Emma Fierke, had died in 1904. When Mr. Yahr passed away on February 10, 1935, he was buried in his family vault at West Side Cemetery with his first wife.

Martha lived on until the noon hour of Sunday, March 14, 1937, when she succumbed at the Ripon Municipal Hospital after a lengthy illness. On January 21 she had fallen, broken her hip and sustained numerous other injuries. Following funeral services at St. John's Lutheran Church on Wednesday, her body was taken to Princeton City Cemetery and placed beside that of Dr. Wendlandt's.

In paying her tribute, the local paper characterized her as "a woman of general impulses" who "never forgot the hospitable ways of the pioneer." "The stranger, even though a beggar," said the editor, "never failed to find shelter if he sought it at her hands, and she was at home by the bedside of the sick and delighted in all kinds of neighborly offices." "Truth," he vouched, "was the inspiration of her life and by kindness she exemplified its great worth." Indeed, she must have been a wonderful wife to both Dr. Wendlandt and Mr. Yahr. "Flowers, not thorns, sunshine, not shadow, did she scatter everywhere," the newspaper declared.

Although Martha sleeps beneath a rather small and plain

headstone, it is hoped that the pages of this chapter will scatter her memory in a much wider circle. She deserves to be remembered forever.[136]

Hedwig Hermine (Richter) Wendlandt (1857-1891) lived in the Lincoln Home with her husband, Dr. Wendlandt, from 1879 to 1883. Photo courtesy of William I. Richter. No photograph of Dr. Wendlandt has been discovered.

This is Dr. Wendlandt's tombstone in Princeton City Cemetery. Photo by LaVerne Marshall.

References

111 Hickey, "Own the house. . .," *Jour. Ill. State Hist. Soc.*, LXXIV, 279-296 (Winter, 1981).

112 *Illinois State Journal*, Aug. 1, 1879, p. 1, c. 1, p. 4, c. 2.

113 U.S. Census 1880, Springfield, Sangamon Co., Ill., E.D. 229, p. 3, 11. 36-42; *Gould's Springfield Directory, For 1880-81*, 152.

114 Photo in *Jour. Ill. State Hist. Soc.*, LXXIV, 290-291.

115 *Directory of City of St. Louis 1871*, 685.

116 James Moore Ball, "Dr. Adam Hammer, Surgeon and Apostle of Higher Medical Education," *Jour. Mo. State Medical Assoc.*, VI, 155-177 (Sept., 1909).

117 Faculty Minutes of Missouri Medical College, MSS., Archives, Washington Univ. School of Medicine, St. Louis, Mo.

118 *Annual Announcement Mo. Medical College, 1873*, 16, *ibid.*

119 *Babeuf's Directory of Springfield, Illinois* (Springfield: Ill. Journal Co., 1875), 150, 131, 160; *Springfield City Directory 1877-78*, 106.

120 *Lincoln Centennial Assoc. Papers 1925*, 49.

121 U.S. Census 1880, Springfield, Sangamon Co., Ill., E.D. 223, p. 8, 11. 22-25; *Springfield City Directory 1877-78*, 91; *Springfield City Directory 1889-90*, 261; Receipt No. 9443, Auditor's Receipt Book 1890-91, MS., Illinois State Archives.

122 Register of Physicians and Accoucheurs in the State of Illinois, IV, 187, MS., Illinois State Archives.

123 Wendlandt's note added to his application for license from Wisconsin Board of Medical Examiners, Series 1606, Box 7, State Hist. Soc. of Wis. Registration of Marriage, No. 307, IV, 154, MS., Register of Deeds, Manitowoc Co., Wis.

124 *Gould's Springfield Directory For 1880-81*, 206, 244.

125 U.S. Census 1880, Springfield, Sangamon Co., Ill., E.D. 229, p. 17, 11. 10-12.

126 *Business and Family Directory of Springfield, Ill., 1881-82*, 104.

127 *Springfield City Directory 1887-88* (Springfield: J.E. Fitzpatrick, 1887), 283, 328, 386. The Seebergers opened this store about the same time as Wendlandt engaged the office space above them.

128 Tombstones in Evergreen Cemetery; *Daily Illinois State Register*, Feb. 13, 1891, p. 5, c. 2.

129 Wendlandt's note added to his application for license from Wisconsin Board of Medical Examiners.

130 *Springfield City Directory 1894*, 472, 562.

131 Marriage License, County Clerk, Cook Co.; U.S. Census 1900, Princeton, Green Lake Co., Wis., E.D. 59, p. 5, 11. 36-37.

132 His phone number at the office was 298; his residence phone was 241. *Springfield City Directory, 1896*, 505, 570, 572.

133 *Springfield City Directory 1898*, 568, 643.

134 Wisconsin Board of Medical Examiners, Applications for Licenses 1897-1907, Series 1606, Box 7, State Hist. Soc. of Wis. His record in Register of Physicians and Accoucheurs in the State of Illinois, IV, 187, gives the date he left Illinois. LaVerne Marshall discovered the date he purchased property by examining deed records in Princeton, Wis.

135 Death Record, I, 42, Green Lake Co., Wis.; *Princeton Times-Republic*, Oct. 21, 1909, p. 1, c. 1; tombstones in Princeton City Cemetery.

136 *The Princeton Republic*, Feb. 21, 1935, p. 1, c. 2; Mar. 18, 1937, p. 1, c. 2.

O.H. and Lida A. Oldroyd
from Benham, *Life of Osborn H. Oldroyd.*

The Oldroyds

“I moved in as [Wendlandt] moved out, which was in 1883,” recalled O.H. Oldroyd on April 15, 1925. He promised to pay Robert Lincoln $25 per month as rent money.[137] And there he resided with his family for approximately ten years.

Osborn Hamiline Ingham Oldroyd had been born not far from Mt. Vernon, Ohio, on July 31, 1842. His parents, William and Mary (Singer) Oldroyd,[138] had named him so that his initials would spell out his native state: OHIO.[139] Yet Osborn never used Ingham when writing his full name. His paternal grandfather, Charles Oldroyd, had manufactured quality woolen blankets in Huddersfield, Yorkshire, England. There, the family name was spelled “Holdroyd,” but when Charles and Jane brought their family to the United States in 1809, they dropped the “H” from their last name as soon as they settled as farmers in Clinton Township of Wayne County, Ohio.[140] (The British rarely pronounce the “h” if it is the first letter of a word. So the change was no doubt made for the benefit of American pronunciation.) Their son William had been born in England and came with them. He later married Mary Singer, who had been born in Pennsylvania, and this union produced at least two children: Osborn and Olivia.[141]

For some reason, Mary (Singer) Oldroyd and her two children resided alone on a farm with her father-in-law and mother-in-law for a number of years. She did not join her husband, William, in Mt. Vernon, Knox County, Ohio, until sometime after 1850.[142] At that time, the children began attending the common schools of Mt. Vernon. Upon reaching eighteen, Osborn started up a little news stand in that city.[143] But within a year, the Civil War erupted, and Osborn enlisted on October 15, 1861, as a Private in Company E of the 20th Ohio Infantry Regiment. Before he reached his twenty-first birthday, he advanced to become the Fifth Sergeant of his company. At Raymond, Mississippi, he received wounds yet temporarily took over command of the company when his superior officers were either killed or wounded. However, he never received a commission and was mustered out of the service as a Veteran Sergeant on July 16, 1865.[144] Nevertheless, Oldroyd later appropriated the rank of "Captain" and passed himself off as a former officer.[145]

After having served his Country well, Oldroyd returned home. He probably resumed his news agency. Better positions, however, were available to veterans if they played politics and petitioned for them. Within two years, Oldroyd secured the post of Assistant Steward at the Central Branch of the National Home for Disabled Soldiers at Dayton, Ohio. He advanced his career by becoming the Steward for the Southern Ohio Lunatic Asylum in November of 1869. He lived on the grounds and disbursed the money for this institution—also in Dayton.

In the course of his social life in Dayton, Osborn Oldroyd met Lida A. Stoneberger, daughter of William and Josephine B. Stoneberger. Lida's parents had moved to Dayton from Pennsylvania in 1836. Lida was born in Dayton on January 5, 1845, although O.H. Oldroyd once told Carl W. Schaefer that his wife—like Mary (Todd) Lincoln—had been born in Lexington, Kentucky.[146] It would seem that Oldroyd was given to fabricating a few fantasies when ever he discoursed upon family history. Lida, evidently, remained in Dayton when her parents moved on to Springfield, Illinois, about 1862. A skilled millwright, William Stoneberger found employment with Berriman & Rippon at Ninth and Adams in Springfield. This firm manufactured steam engines, saw mills, sugar mills, columns, pilasters, caps, sills, school desks, etc.[147]

When Lida and Osborn decided to get married, they took their vows in her parents' home. Rev. John H. Barrows conducted the ceremony on April 23, 1873.[148] As soon as their honeymoon was over, the newlyweds returned to Dayton, Ohio. In that city their first child was born.[149]

However, in July of 1874, the Oldroyds moved west to Springfield, Illinois, to be in the company of her family.

The Oldroyds took up residence in a rented house at 618 North Fifth Street; the Stonebergers lived at 617. Since William Stoneberger could do carpentry and woodworking, Oldroyd determined to erect a factory where he and his in-laws could do manufacturing. (His brother-in-law, Louis A. Stoneberger, also labored as a carpenter.) Fitting action to thoughts, Oldroyd had constructed for himself a one-story brick building on the west side of the alley between Fourth and Fifth and Carpenter and Union. In it he installed a planing machine, a broomhandle lathe, a circular saw, and a spoke machine. These ran from shafts and belting powered by a steam engine. Connected to this structure was a steam-dry house heated by a boiler. Its address was 618-620 North 4th, and the outlet for their products was a store at 118-120 North 5th. In his shop, which opened about January 25, 1875, Oldroyd turned out wagon and carriage woodwork, spokes, washboards, clothespins, stair balusters, table legs, packing boxes, hammer handles, and all sorts of scroll sawing, planing and turning.[150] He even produced ball bats, rolling pins and potato mashers. One could purchase oak lumber there, too.

Alas, Oldroyd operated on borrowed money, and his "wooden-ware manufactory" could not pay all its bills. To stay open, he formed a partnership with Elon P. House on September 30, 1876. About thirty years of age, House had been born in New York and came to Springfield in 1863 where he ran a hardware store with Benjamin F. Fox. Even this financial succor could not save Oldroyd, and he filed for bankruptcy on December 5, 1876. Later (in October of 1886), John Carroll Power, Custodian of the Lincoln Tomb and a rival for recognition in the field of Lincolniana, accused Oldroyd of not having declared his Lincoln collection when he took bankruptcy. (Since 1860, Oldroyd had assembled Lincolniana.) But in all fairness to the accused, it must be pointed out that on Schedule B, No. 2, "Personal Property," Oldroyd did list "Books, prints & pictures" valued at $200. That was his Lincoln collection at that time.[151]

Although Oldroyd took personal bankruptcy, the firm of Oldroyd & House continued to function. O.H. Oldroyd ran the business alone "under a lease from Oldroyd & House." Apparently, he earned a living in this shop for several years. Be that as it may, by 1880 Osborn Oldroyd had become a bookkeeper for John Bressmer's dry goods store which boasted of two entrances to this prestigious establishment: 530 East Adams and 270 S. Sixth. The Oldroyds also moved to a rented property at 1101 S. Seventh. Due to his love for the Sixteenth President, Osborn was gradually getting closer to the ultimate "shrine" at Eighth and Jackson.[152]

Next, Osborn attempted to operate a sweets shop with his brother-in-law, Frank S. Stoneberger. As Stoneberger & Oldroyd, Confectioners, they opened a store about the year

1881 at 120 South Sixth Street, on the east side of the Public Square. Actually, it appears to have been mostly an ice cream parlor with other desserts available. Although a carpenter by trade, another brother-in-law, Louis A. Stoneberger, clerked there with Oldroyd, too.[153]

Always interested in literary matters, Sgt. Oldroyd had kept a diary during the Civil War. Thus, as he stood watching the memorial service at the Lincoln Tomb on the morning of April 15, 1880, Oldroyd determined to compile a book which would add "luster to the fame of" Abraham Lincoln. At the same time, he hoped that such a publication would earn enough money to build a "Memorial Hall" to house his growing Lincoln collection.[154] So, in addition to keeping books for Bressmer's or dipping ice cream, Oldroyd petitioned notable people to contribute essays for his proposed volume. He succeeded in obtaining manuscripts from such leading figures as Isaac N. Arnold, Charles Francis Adams, Ambrose E. Burnside, John Bright, Cassius M. Clay, Schuyler Colfax, Jesse W. Fell, U.S. Grant, Wm. H. Herndon, Richard J. Oglesby, Joshua F. Speed, W.O. Stoddard, Leonard W. Volk, and many, many others who had actually known the great President.

To these statements, Oldroyd added samples from A. Lincoln's own writings, speeches or sayings. He finished his task by July of 1882, and later that year his large tome of 571 pages, plus 28 pages of introductory material, came off the presses of G.W. Carleton & Co. at New York. It bore an impressive title, *The Lincoln Memorial: Album-Immortelles. . .*and was also distributed in London by S. Low, Son & Co. "SOLD ONLY BY SUBSCRIPTION," said the title page.

In truth, O.H. Oldroyd had made a most significant contribution to the history of Lincoln. Even though many of the pages contain mere flowery platitudes, a few of Lincoln's close friends wrote wonderful reminiscences for Oldroyd's Album. No serious Lincoln scholar today can afford to ignore this work.

Sometime in 1882 or 1883, the Charles D. Arnold house became vacant. Mr. Arnold had inherited this dwelling in 1879, and it stood at 500 South Eighth Street (Lot No. 1, Block 11), being on the southeast corner of 8th and Jackson. Thus, it sat just south of the Lincoln home, across Jackson, with a perfect view of the sacred house and lot where the Lincolns had lived for nearly seventeen years. Needless to recount, the Oldroyds rented the Arnold place immediately.[155]

Then, as luck would have it, Dr. Wendlandt gave up his lease of the Lincoln residence sometime in 1883. As soon as Oldroyd discovered that the Wendlandts were departing, he quickly rented the famous wooden dwelling from Clinton Conkling, Robert Lincoln's agent. Osborn, Lida, and their daughter, Daisy, transported all their earthly possessions across the street to the hallowed spot and reëstablished housekeeping.

Such a move certainly boosted the spirits of the Oldroyds, because, as a businessman, Osborn had experienced scant success. Oh, his book sold well enough, but his confectionery and ice cream enterprise failed miserably. His brother-in-law and partner, Frank Stoneberger, removed to Chicago in an attempt to secure employment, and their stand on the east side of the Square disappeared. Not even the city directory carried Oldroyd's name in 1884. Nonetheless, the fertile mind of Osborn had formulated a plan to earn a living.

With his expanding collection of Lincolniana spread out all over the front and back parlors, Oldroyd threw open the Lincoln home to visitors and charged them a fee to enter. In recalling these events in February of 1925, however, Oldroyd piously stated that he admitted "visitors free during that time." Two months afterwards, he again repeated this falsehood, saying, "I never took a penny for admissions during my occupancy of ten years."[156] Oldroyd had even asked Robert Lincoln's permission to charge for entrance to the home, and Robert replied that he "had no objection to his doing so." Only John Carroll Power at the Lincoln Tomb voiced a complaint; he, too, you see, had a competitive assemblage of relics for the public to view—for a 25¢ "donation," naturally.[157]

Despite the fact that Oldroyd demanded admission money from tourists who wished to view the Lincoln home (and probably attempted to sell his book or prints of the house to them, also), he fell behind in his rent to Robert Lincoln. After August 1, 1885, Osborn ceased to remit his monthly payments.[158] Instead of paying on his lease, it seems reasonable to assume that Oldroyd spent every nickel he could glean to enlarge his collection of Lincoln artifacts, statues, photos, etc.

In an attempt to supplement his precarious income, Oldroyd reverted to a trade which he had followed prior to the Civil War. He inaugurated a book store about 1885 at 222 South Sixth. There, he purveyed books, newspapers and stationery,[159] while his wife and daughter, no doubt, ushered visitors through their home. A gifted conversationalist, Oldroyd entertained his customers and eked out a slim livelihood. He also sold—in person and by mail—a box of "relics" from the home. These were small pieces of wood, etc., removed during remodeling.

A consummate politician, Oldroyd had established one goal for himself about the time his book rolled from the press: get the Lincoln home established as a State memorial so that he could reside there, earn a salary as the custodian, and display his collection. Somehow he convinced James M. Gregg of Saline County, a Democrat, to offer a resolution in the House of Representatives on March 9, 1883. It stated that "Mr. O.H. Oldroyd, a citizen and resident of Springfield, and the author of the '*Lincoln Memorial Album*,' and the collector during the last twenty years of nearly two thousand books, medals, pictures, badges, sermons, eulogies and mementos of

Abraham Lincoln, is desirous of putting [them] into some permanent place for preservation, where the people can see and know what the nations have done for the honor of Illinois' great statesman. . . ." It further directed the Governor, John M. Hamilton, a Republican, to "correspond with Hon. Robert T. Lincoln, and ascertain for what price the State of Illinois can purchase the old homestead of Abraham Lincoln. . . ." The Senate concurred on March 13. Being a joint resolution, it did not require the Governor's signature to become law.[160]

Completely surprised by the passage of this resolution, Mr. Robert Lincoln replied to Gov. Hamilton on April 9, saying simply, "I have determined not to part with the ownership of the property." Again, in 1884, the General Assembly considered purchasing the house, but on June 9 Robert told Attorney General James McCartney, a Republican, that if he "should think it proper to part with the property to the state, there would need be no appropriation for its purchase from me." Such a statement only encouraged Oldroyd when he learned of it. He continued to lobby.

Nothing transpired in 1885, but two years later Oldroyd had success. He approached Rep. Charles Bogardus, a Republican from Ford County, and asked him to shepherd a measure through the House.[161] Accordingly, on March 9, 1887, Bogardus offered a resolution which called for five members to "confer with the Hon. Robert T. Lincoln, or his representative, Mr. Clinton L. Conkling, of 205 South Fifth Street, Springfield, in relation to the property commonly known as the 'Lincoln Residence,' and upon what terms or conditions Mr. Lincoln will convey said property to the State of Illinois." The House adopted it immediately, and later that day, the Speaker, William F. Calhoun, appointed the committee: Bogardus, Alfred H. Jones of Crawford, Henry Decker of Cook, Edgar S. Browne of La Salle, and Wesford Taggart of Douglas.[162]

This special House committee met with Conkling at the Leland Hotel in Springfield, and the latter reported to Robert Lincoln on April 25. Although again astonished by this action, Robert nevertheless responded kindly by letter five days later. "If the State will offer to preserve the house as an object of public interest," Robert avowed, "all question will be avoided and you may say to the chairman that upon such an offer being made I will convey the property to the State without compensation."[163]

Rep. Bogardus introduced H.B. 848 on May 25, 1887, to acquire the Lincoln home. It passed both houses, and Gov. Richard J. Oglesby signed it into law on June 16, 1887. This legislation created a board of Lincoln Homestead Trustees to "receive a conveyance from Robert T. Lincoln and his wife, of Chicago, of the homestead of the late Abraham Lincoln. . . ." The Governor, Secretary of State, Auditor, Treasurer and Superintendent of Public Instruction made up this board. These officers should "have full authority over and control of said homestead." They would employ a custodian and keep the premises in repair.[164]

Robert Lincoln learned of this law not from the General Assembly but from the newspapers. Despite this fact, he and his wife, Mary Harlan Lincoln, signed a deed to the Lincoln Homestead Trustees on July 8, 1887, saying that "said Homestead shall be forever kept in good repair and free of access to the public." After being duly notarized in Chicago, the instrument was carried to Springfield and recorded in Sangamon County.[165] The Trustees accepted the gift on July 19, binding themselves, and their successors in office, to keep the property "in good repair and free of access to the public."

Robert Lincoln no doubt breathed a sign of relief. No longer would he have taxes and expenses to pay on the home. Too, he had not received a penny from Oldroyd for nearly two years. Privately, Robert had previously summed up his feelings about him. "I suppose that in fact my present tenant is a dead beat and that this whole proceeding is expected practically to provide him a home free of rent," Robert expostulated, "but I do not think that is a matter of any concern to me." What Robert most regretted was feeling himself "the victim of an imposition." Yet he never wanted Conkling to take legal measures to collect the rent from Oldroyd. He had cautioned his agent not to take a chattel mortgage on Oldroyd's "traps." Robert simply hated publicity of this nature.[166]

Meeting in the office of the Governor on August 12, 1887, the Lincoln Homestead Trustees first elected officers.

With Gov. Richard J. Oglesby's approval, the State of Illinois acquired the Lincoln Home in 1887. As a Major General in the Civil War, Oglesby had served under President Lincoln when he was Commander-in-Chief. Photo by "Doc" Helm.

Oglesby became Chairman, and the Auditor, Charles P. Swigert, Secretary. Because the position of custodian offered a lucrative opportunity, sixteen applicants applied for the post. "After careful consideration of the question, on the 29th day of August, 1887, Mr. O.H. Oldroyd, of Springfield, Illinois, the owner of the collection of relics, curiosities and memorials contained in said homestead, was selected as custodian, and his salary fixed at $1,000 per annum." Oldroyd entered into a contract with the Trustees on October 3 that year. He agreed "to keep on exhibition, open and free of access to the public during all reasonable hours upon weekdays, the curiosities and relics there collected and belongings to said Oldroyd."[167] So, the Custodian did not even have to open the home on weekends when many visitors would be in town.

Oldroyd's official address may have been 430 S. 8th, but actually it might have been called "Easy Street." Within a year, he gave up his news agency. His wife's parents, William and Josephine Stoneberger, moved in, as did two of her brothers, Charles P. and Louis A. Stoneberger. Charles clerked at John Bressmer's, and Louis, nicknamed "Shorty," served as an "attaché" in the St. Nicholas Hotel, managing the dining room service and the menu cards.[168] Therefore, seven people resided in the Lincoln home. One might have also accused Oldroyd of operating a "boarding-house." Without doubt, he certainly collected some rent and board money from those of his in-laws who were working.

William Stoneberger died in the Lincoln homestead on March 10, 1888, at the age of 77. His funeral took place there two days later. His widow, Josephine, succumbed in the same place on August 15, 1888, at the age of 78. Her funeral likewise was held there two days afterward.[169]

When the Oldroyds took over the Lincoln property, they had found that "the house and grounds were in a most dilapidated condition." Even though Osborn declared that he immediately "spent all my leisure time and, at my own expense, to get the historic house and grounds in a respectable condition," he probably did very little until 1888.[170] At that time, the State of Illinois authorized the Custodian to spend $2,800 which had been appropriated for repair and maintenance. L.W. Coe painted the exterior of the residence and also the kitchen and dining room. Two carpenters, Otto Redeker and Ole K. Nelson, labored for a total of 19 days doing repairs. J.S. Culver redid steps, etc. Rooms were papered, pipes fixed, sod laid, etc. Other workmen plastered ceilings, repaired chimneys. George Smith worked on the barn and fence. Rhodes & Bro. did unspecified carpenter work to the tune of $58.26.[171] Oldroyd reminisced in 1925 that "there was a little old stable" standing upon the rear of the Lincoln lot when he became the renter. He, in ignorance of historic preservation, ordered it torn down and another one built to replace it. Knowing this fact, one could easily guess that George Smith, for $11.50, dismantled this ancient and historic stable (or barn) at this particular time. In it, Abraham

Lincoln had milked his own cow, curried and fed his own horses. It, too, had figured largely in the home life of the tall Lawyer.

Refurbishing continued in 1889. The Culver Marble & Stone Company of Springfield laid brick walks, installed curbing, graded and sodded around the stone walks, made a hydrant platform, put in hitching posts, a horse block, etc. Buck & McKee charged the State $180 for carpenter work on the barn. J.H. Barkley & Co. furnished a "Palace King furnace" for heating.[172] Naturally, many of these items had never been there in the Lincolns' time, and their appearance altered the property somewhat.

Early in 1890, Oldroyd removed the dead apple tree which had stood in the Lincoln yard for years and replaced the famous elm trees on the lot. The yard was resodded, too. L.W. Coe painted the kitchen and the "foundation on the front wall of Lincoln Homestead." He later painted the tin roof on the back building. The coping was replaced for $38.50, and E.F. Gehlman repaired and replaced the fence. As the year passed, laborers worked on the roof and the gutters.[173]

When President and Mrs. Benjamin Harrison visited Springfield on May 14, 1891, Oldroyd took part in a rare treat. The Presidential Special arrived at 9:15 a.m., and Custodian Oldroyd marched in the parade. But Harrison discovered that time would not permit his visiting the Lincoln home. However, John Wanamaker, Postmaster General, and Jeremiah M. Rusk, Secretary of Agriculture, paid a call at the historic residence of Lincoln.[174]

Shortly after the Oldroyds had finally refurbished the Lincoln residence completely to their liking, disaster struck them. Since 1857, Republicans had held the Governor's chair, but on November 8, 1892, the Democrats swept the state offices with John Peter Altgeld defeating the incumbent, Gov. Joseph W. Fifer, by nearly 23,000 votes. As soon as Altgeld was sworn into office on January 10, 1893, he dispatched a special messenger to inform Oldroyd, a strong Republican, that he had approximately two weeks to vacate the premises.[175] Altgeld evidently felt that he could rule the other Trustees because they were all Democrats, too.

Wm. H. Hinrichsen, David Gore, Rufus N. Ramsey and Henry Raab met with Altgeld on April 12, 1893. They elected Altgeld President and Hinrichsen, Secretary. Next, they fired Oldroyd and picked Mr. Herman Hofferkamp to replace him as of April 15. As a further slap at the departing Oldroyd, the Trustees decreed that the Custodian could not charge any fee for "showing the building," nor could he "sell any picture, relic or any other article; in fact he is not allowed to receive money from visitors in any shape or for any purpose." They kept the salary at $1,000.[176]

This startling turn of events struck Robert Lincoln —a staunch Republican—like a tidal wave. He had informed Gov. Altgeld prior to this action that if a change had to be made, he preferred his cousin, Albert Stevenson Edwards, for the post. Edwards, Robert disclosed, was not only a

Democrat but also had served his country during the Civil War. Robert had not lobbied to remove Oldroyd, as some writers hinted years later.

"Petty and Disgraceful Partisanship," shrieked the headline of a local Republican newspaper. "It has been supposed that the spoils hunters among the hungry Democracy would perhaps be foiled by the force of public sentiment in their efforts to break into at least one of the places which accidentally came into their control at the November election, but it seems that no place is too sacred and none too petty to be prostituted to partisan purposes under a pretended 'reform' administration," the editor declared with vigor. "The removal of Captain O.H. Oldroyd as custodian of the Lincoln Home in this city and the appointment in his place of a petty Democratic politician and persistent place-seeker," the editor fumed, "means much more than the displacement of a Republican to provide for a Democrat." Altgeld's action had stripped the home of a Lincoln collection which visitors enjoyed viewing, explained the angry editor. The new Custodian, he pointed out candidly to his readers, "will be provided with a salary and a house to live in at the expense of the state, but will have nothing to show to those who visit the Home and consequently little to do." Nor, he reflected, had Hofferkamp ever taken an interest in the Lincoln shrine. "The new appointee," jeered the irate editor, "lived for years within sight of the old homestead and watched it going to decay without one single sentimental or patriotic impulse to guard it and preserve it."

When interviewed by the press, Oldroyd said glumly, "I have no definite plans for the future." He speculated that he might take his collection to Chicago and exhibit it at the World's Columbian Exposition slated to open that summer. He further revealed to the reporter that he had not even, as yet, received a formal notice of removal.[177]

Oldroyd's first concern was to secure a temporary storage place for his Lincolniana and a place to live. Dr. Charles Ryan, a physician, had died January 24, 1883, and his house at 430 S. Sixth still remained vacant. It stood on the northeast corner of Sixth and Jackson, just two blocks west of the Lincoln residence. Into it, Oldroyd stashed his vast assemblage.[178] There it remained a few months until the Memorial Association of the District of Columbia asked him to display his collection in the Petersen House at 516 Tenth Street, N.W. Consisting of three storeys and a high basement, it had been constructed by William Petersen, a Swedish tailor, in 1849. And in a humble bedroom of this structure, Pres. Abraham Lincoln had died on the morning of April 15, 1865. He had been carried there from Ford's Theatre which stands just across the way.

On October 17, 1893, Oldroyd opened his exhibit to the public in these quarters which he had rented. Prior to this time, the building stood unoccupied. He showed his artifacts on the first floor and lived in the rooms above. One person estimated that within a few years Oldroyd earned about $10,000 per annum from visitors who paid to see the museum collection.[179] In his spare moments, Oldroyd wrote articles and books on his typewriter and participated diligently in the affairs of the G.A.R. In fact, he won appointment by its Commander-in-Chief to the staff of that patriotic organization of Civil War veterans and promptly announced that he was to be called "Colonel" from thence forward.[180] At long last he had obtained an officer's rank which possessed at least a small semblance of legitimacy.

Once more, Oldroyd began maneuvering to obtain his living quarters free of rent—as he had done back in Springfield. He succeeded, and the United States Government purchased the Petersen House on October 7, 1896.[181] Next, he let it be known that his collection could also be purchased. Years passed before this scheme came to fruition. Finally, Congressman-at-Large Henry R. Rathbone, Jr., a Republican of Chicago, Illinois, sponsored such a bill in Congress. Here, Oldroyd had shrewdly picked a politician with a sentimental attachment to the Lincoln legend. Rep. Rathbone was the son of Maj. Henry R. and Clara (Harris) Rathbone who had sat in the box at Ford's Theatre with the Lincolns on the evening that the President had been shot.[182] After much political pressure and haggling, the measure won approval, and the United States purchased Oldroyd's relics for $50,000 on August 30, 1926.

Two days later, the Government took possession of the collection, and in line of duty the Superintendent of Public

Buildings and Public Parks called to see Oldroyd. This official was none other than Lt. Col. Ulysses S. Grant, III (July 4, 1881-Aug. 29, 1968), grandson of President Grant. He offered to let Oldroyd remain as custodian of the museum, but the "Colonel" declined, saying he was past 84 years of age and tired. Upon hearing this, Col. Grant reached into his pocket, presented Oldroyd with a key to the Petersen House, and invited him to come and go as he liked. That honor Oldroyd did accept. He last visited the Petersen building on July 25, 1930.[183]

Oldroyd had been blessed with an excellent constitution. He liked to walk, and even after he turned sixty, Osborn continued his hikes, sometimes traveling for several hundred miles. He was well past 88 when he died at his residence, 1723 Webster Street, N.W., in Washington, DC, on October 8, 1930. His heart and kidneys had simply given out. The Rev. Jason Noble Pierce, pastor of the First Congregational Church, conducted the funeral three days later. Burial was made in Section T, Lot 232, Site 2 of Rock Creek Cemetery in the Capital City.[184]

Lida A. Oldroyd succumbed on September 21, 1934, and was interred beside her husband. Daisy (Oldroyd) Gordon died November 24, 1942, and was likewise buried with her parents.[185] Because these three family members had resided in the noted home of the Lincolns at Springfield, they must be remembered as part of the Lincoln scenario.

References

137 *Lincoln Centennial Assoc. Papers* 1925, 53-54.

138 Oldroyd's Certificate of Death lists his parents' names, No. 330703, Vital Records Division, Dist. of Columbia, Washington. He, himself, never mentioned their names in his writings.

139 Carl W. Schaefer, "Osborn H. Oldroyd," *Lincoln Herald*, XLVI, 4 (Oct., 1944).

140 Wm. Burton Benham, *Life of Osborn H. Oldroyd* (Washington: Beresford, 1927), 25.

141 U.S. Census 1850, Clinton Twp., Wayne Co., Ohio, p. 12, 11. 14-18.

142 *Ibid.*

143 Benham, *Oldroyd*, 6.

144 *Official Roster of the Soldiers of the State of Ohio in the War of the Rebellion 1861-1866* (Cincinnati: Wilstach Baldwin & Co., 1886), II, 701.

145 *Springfield City Directory. . .1877-78* (Springfield: M.G. Tousley & Co., 1877), 78.

146 Washington (D.C.) *Post*, Oct. 9, 1930, p. 1, c. 3; *Lincoln Herald*, XLVI, 3 (Oct., 1944); *Daily Illinois State Journal*, Aug. 16, 1888, p. 4, c. 1.

147 *Springfield City Directory For 1863*, 38, 41, 127.

148 Marriage Records, IV, 551, License No. 5492, MS., County Clerk's Office Sangamon Co. Bldg., Springfield, Ill. John H. Barrows cannot be identified.

149 U.S. Census 1880, Springfield, Sangamon Co., Ill., E.D. 229, p. 9, 11. 16-18.

150 *Babeuf's Directory of Springfield, Illinois. . .For the Year 1875* (Springfield: Ill. Jour. Co., 1875), 116; *Centennial. . .Directory of Springfield, Illinois* (Springfield: Ill. Jour. Co., 1876), 227; *Springfield City Directory. . .1877-78*, 78, 98.

151 U.S. Census 1880, Springfield, Sangamon Co., Ill., E.D. 229, p. 40, 11. 1-3; *Babeuf's Directory of Springfield, Illinois. . .1874-5*, 79; Petition No. 1857, United States District Court, Southern District of Illinois, MSS., RG 21, Federal Archives & Records Center, Chicago, Ill.; *Jour. Ill. State Hist. Soc.*, LXXIV, 289 (Winter, 1981). On the day that Oldroyd filed for bankruptcy, he assigned his interest to House who continued to own the shop for some time. Oldroyd's financial affairs were not settled until 1880. E.P. House left Springfield in 1886 and eventually ended up in San Francisco where he died in 1894. *Illinois State Journal*, June 15, 1894, p. 5, c. 4.

152 U.S. Census 1880, Springfield, Sangamon Co., Ill., E.D. 229, p. 9, 11. 16-18; *Gould's Springfield Directory, For 1880-81* (Springfield: David B. Gould, n.d.), 35, 156.

153 *Babeuf's Directory of the City of Springfield. . . 1882-3* (Springfield: J. Babeuf, 1882), 176, 219.

154 Osborn H. Oldroyd, ed., *The Lincoln Memorial: Album-Immortelles. . .* (N.Y.: G.W. Carleton & Co., 1882), v.

155 *Lincoln Cent. Assoc. Papers* 1925, 50.

156 *Ibid.* 50-51, 54.

157 *Jour. Ill. State Hist. Soc.*, LXXIV, 289, 292; Power, *Abraham Lincoln*, 452.

158 *Jour. Ill. State Hist. Soc.*, LXXIV, 294.

159 *Babeuf's Directory of the City of Springfield. . . 1886-7* (Springfield: J. Babeuf, 1886), 212; *Springfield City Directory* (Springfield: J.E. Fitzpatrick, 1887), 241, 381. When Oldroyd died, an editor in Springfield recalled him as the operator of a book store there. *Illinois State Journal*, Oct. 10, 1930, p. 1, c. 7.

160 *Jour. of the House of Representatives of the 33rd G.A.* (Springfield: H.W. Rokker, 1883), 356, 372; *Laws of the State of Illinois. . .* (Springfield: H.W. Rokker, 1883), 188.

161 *Lincoln Cent. Assoc. Papers 1925*, 51.

162 *Jour. of the House of Representatives of the 35th G.A.* (Springfield: Springfield Printing Co., 1888), 385, 394.

163 *Jour. Ill. State Hist. Soc.*, LXXIV, 292-294.

164 *Laws of the State of Illinois. . .* (Springfield: H.W. Rokker, 1887), 39-40.

165 Deed Record, LXXX, 299, MS., Recorder of Deeds Office, Sangamon Co. Bldg.

166 *Jour. Ill. State Hist. Soc.*, LXXIV, 292-293.

167 *Jour. House of Representatives 36th G.A.* (Springfield: Springfield Printing Co., 1889), 171-174.

168 *Springfield City Directory 1889-90*, 226, 283, 402. L.A. Stoneberger died in Springfield on October 19, 1915, at the age of 81. C.P. Stoneberger died in Chicago on November 16, 1916, at the age of nearly 69. Both are buried in Oak Ridge Cemetery at Springfield with their parents. *Illinois State Journal*, Oct. 20, 1915, p. 7, c. 2; Death Certificate No. 31618, Dept. of Public Health, State of Ill.

169 *Daily Illinois State Journal*, Mar. 12, 1888, p. 4, c. 5; Aug. 16, 1888, p. 4, c. 1.

170 *Lincoln Cent. Assoc. Papers* 1925., 53.

171 *Jour. House of Rep. 36th G.A.*, 174.

172 Auditor's Receipt Book 1889-90, Nos. 5542, 5612, 6377, 6469, 6986, 6987, MS., Illinois State Archives.

173 Auditor's Receipt Book 1890-91, Nos. 9152, 9315, 9673, 290, 364, 642, 1020, MS., *ibid.*

174 *Daily Illinois State Journal*, May 15, 1891, p. 8, c. 1.

175 *Lincoln Cent. Assoc. Papers* 1925, 51.

176 *Reports to the General Assembly of Illinois 1894* (Springfield: Phillips Bros., 1898), X, No. 12, pp. 1-5.

177 *Illinois State Journal*, Apr. 13, 1893, p. 2, c. 2; p. 4, cc. 1-2.

178 *Lincoln Cent. Assoc. Papers 1925*, 51; *Babeuf's Directory of the City of Springfield, Illinois 1884-5*, 22; *Directory of Springfield 1882-3*, 198.

179 *Illinois State Journal*, Oct. 10, 1930, p. 1, c. 7; Stanley W. McClure, *Ford's Theatre and the House Where Lincoln Died* (Washington: National Park Service, 1969), 23.

180 Washington *Evening Star*, Oct. 9, 1930, A-3, cc. 2-3; *Lincoln Herald*, XLVI, 5, (Oct., 1944).

181 McClure, *Ford's Theatre. . .* , 23. The Oldroyds' only granddaughter, Josephine (Oldroyd) Thiefenthaler, died in the Petersen House on Feb. 20, 1908, the very anniversary of "Willie" Lincoln's death at the

White House: Feb. 20, 1862. She had been born on July 17, 1896. Benham, *Oldroyd*, 28; Certificate of Death No. 178497, Dist. of Columbia.

182 *Blue Book of the State of Illinois 1925-1926* (Springfield: State of Ill., 1925), 70.

183 McClure, *Ford's Theater. . .*, 23; Washington *Evening Star*, Oct. 9, 1930, p. A-3, cc. 2-3. U.S. Grant, III, advanced to the rank of Major General before his retirement.

184 Certificate of Death No. 330703, Vital Records Division, District of Columbia; Washington *Evening Star*, Oct. 9, 1930, p. A-3, cc. 2-3; Washington *Post*, Oct. 9, 1930, p. 1, c. 3.

185 Burial records at Rock Creek Cemetery. Daisy was the widow of Alexander Gordon and had lived at 2651 Sixteenth Street, N.W. Mr. Gordon had worked for the Washington *Star*. At her death, Daisy left a stepson, Raymond A. Gordon of Washington, D.C., and a stepdaughter-in-law, Mrs. Gertrude Latimer of Parkersburg, West Virginia. Washington *Post*, Nov. 26, 1942, p. 15 B, cc.1, 3.

The House of Abraham After 1893

Herman Hofferkamp succeeded Oldroyd as the Custodian. He—like his benefactor, Gov. Altgeld—had been born in Germany. Hofferkamp's native city was Hanover where he had come into the world on October 26, 1842, the son of John Herman Hofferkamp. His mother's name is unknown. While yet in his teens, Herman arrived in Springfield, Illinois, and soon found employment in the drug store of Thos. J.V. Owen at No. 10 on the south side of the Public Square. During the Civil War, he enlisted on February 28, 1862, as a Private in Company F, Tenth Cavalry Regiment, Illinois Volunteers. The enrolling officer set him down as being 5' 8" tall, with light hair, light complexion and blue eyes. Because of his experience with medicine, he was transferred the following month to the non-commissioned staff of the Regiment as Hospital Steward. He received his honorable discharge on February 28, 1865.[186]

Upon returning home, Herman resumed his clerkship in the drug store. That fall, on his birthday (October 26, 1865), he married Rachael Burns. The Rev. Joseph Costa, pastor of the Catholic Church on the northeast corner of Seventh and Monroe, performed this sacrament for them. The bride was the daughter of Michael and Katherine Burns and seems to have been born in Scotland on March 25, 1844.[187]

For approximately six years, Herman operated a livery business with his brother, John H. Hofferkamp, Jr. But eventually he struck off on his own and took over the American Livery, Sale and Feed Stables at the rear of the Post Office near Monroe Street.[188] Becoming politically minded, Herman ran for Coroner of Sangamon County and won election on November 6, 1888. Unfortunately for him, however, the Democratic Party did not slate him for reelection, and his commission expired November 18, 1892.[189] Therefore, as a lame duck, he needed a political appointment and received it from Gov. Altgeld.

When appointed Custodian of the Lincoln homestead at a salary of $1,000 per year, Hofferkamp resided at 507 South Eighth Street, on the west side of the street and two houses south of Jackson. So, the Hofferkamps had but a short distance to shift their belongings when they took over the Lincoln shrine on April 15, 1893. Once more, the Lincoln residence gave rent-free shelter to a sizeable family. In addition to Herman and Rachael, there were their sons, Charles Edward, about 24 and a clerk at Henson Robinson & Co.; and Harry, about 20 and a clerk at Hall & Herrick; and their daughter, Mary E., about 14 and a student.[190]

Having been stung severely by the editorial in the *Illinois State Journal* of April 13, 1893, the new Board of Trustees for the Lincoln Homestead hastened to assemble artifacts for tourists to view. By January 10, 1895, they reported that "Quite a number of authentic relics, valuable for their association with Mr. Lincoln's past life, have been obtained by donation, and have been placed in the homestead as the property of the State. . . ." They also hired R.F. Kinsella to make numerous cosmetic repairs to the property. He repainted the outside of the entire house, papered three bedrooms, the dining and sitting room, the "Memorial room," and the kitchen. He also executed nine feet of gold lettering, probably in the Memorial Room. In addition, he papered the ceiling in the parlor as well as the closet and pantry. R.H. Armbruster installed an awning, and this is probably the one seen in some later photographs. Of course, the Lincolns never had one. The Trustees also repaired the fence, did some plastering in the rooms and patched the roof.[191]

Altgeld proved to be a most unpopular Governor, being extremely liberal and even pardoning the "Haymarket Anarchists." Then, too, he held office during a severe depression marred further by much labor unrest. When he ran for reelection on November 3, 1896, John R. Tanner, a Civil War veteran and a Republican, defeated him by 113,381 votes. Quickly, Altgeld became the "Eagle Forgotten."

This turn of events spelled doom for Hofferkamp. Robert

Albert and Josephine Edwards served as Custodians of the Lincoln Home at Robert T. Lincoln's insistence. Albert Edwards wrote on February 20, 1897, that "Mrs. Abraham Lincoln was insane from the time of her husband['s] death until her own death." Furthermore, he stated that Robert Lincoln had asked his wife, Josephine Edwards, to nurse and cared for Mary Todd Lincoln while she resided with the Ninian W. Edwards family in Springfield. SC923, MS., Ill. State Hist. Lib. These photos are from J.L. Pickering, *The Illinois Capital Illustrated* (Springfield: *Illinois State Register*, 1898), 106.

Lincoln called upon Tanner within a few days after the election and expressed his wish that the Lincoln house receive a permanent custodian who would not be subject to "political favor." Although Robert had thought it "very proper" that Oldroyd be continued in the home after it had become State property back in 1887, Hofferkamp's appointment by the Democrats turned out to be "most unpleasant" to him as the son of Abraham Lincoln and a strong Republican. It had probably been Custodian Hofferkamp who once thoughtlessly displayed a photo of John Wilkes Booth on the Lincoln mantel. Quite naturally, somebody informed Robert of this faux pas, and he later complained of it to a relative in Springfield. Robert again asked that Albert S. Edwards be given the position.[192]

Edwards himself indited a letter to Samuel M. Inglis, the Superintendent of Public Instruction and a Republican, on November 23, 1896. He told the Superintendent that he possessed a letter from Robert Lincoln saying, "I certainly hope that you may be appointed and I shall say so very earnestly if I am consulted & you may use my name to that effect." When no positive action to his plea took place, many prominent citizens of Springfield signed a petition in February of 1897, asking that Edwards be hired for the post.[193]

Still no decision came from the Trustees. They perhaps objected to picking a known Democrat even if R.T. Lincoln was his first cousin. Finally, after five months, they notified Hofferkamp that he must go. On June 30, 1897, at 2 p.m.,

Hofferkamp held an auction to sell "a lot of relics of Abraham Lincoln which he has had on exhibition at the late Lincoln Home." B.F. Wright cried the sale.[194] How strange to dispose of items which the Trustees had boasted in 1895 were "the property of the State!" On the following day, Herman moved his family out of the Lincoln homestead and back into their own home at 507 South Eighth.[195]

Rachael Hofferkamp died at her home on December 27, 1919, as the result of a cerebral hemorrhage. In three months she would have been 76. Two days later, burial took place in Oak Ridge Cemetery.[196]

Just after six p.m. on October 7, 1922, Herman Hofferkamp penciled a note saying, "I have been in ill health for three years and am tired of living." Upon finishing it, he stepped down into the basement of his son's hardware store at 627 E. Adams, put a caliber .32 revolver to his head and pulled the trigger. By 6:05 he was dead at the age of 80. Like A. Lincoln, he had been killed by a bullet wound to the head. He, too, was buried in Oak Ridge.[197]

On July 1, 1897, the Edwards clan occupied the old Lincoln property. But the stipend had been reduced to $600 per year.[198] It would seem that they paid a price for being Democrats in a Republican administration.

Albert Stevenson Edwards, son of Ninian Wirt and Elizabeth P. (Todd) Edwards, started life at Springfield, Illinois, on December 16, 1839. In the Civil War, he worked for the Commissary Department, evidently as a civilian, at

Camp Douglas in Chicago and at Cairo. Right in the middle of this bloody conflict, he married Josephine E. Remann, daughter of Henry C. and Mary B. (Black) Remann. She had been born in Vandalia, Illinois, on April 28, 1842. They exchanged their nuptial vows on June 3, 1863, in Springfield.[199]

At the time that Albert received his appointment as Custodian of the Lincoln residence, he and his wife lived at 415 South Fifth (three houses south of Capitol Avenue) with their family. Albert kept books for Henry W. Rokker, a printer, publisher and binder with a plant at 309-311 S. Fifth. Edwards had worked there since the War. Two of their four children remained at home with them: Georgie H. Edwards and Ninian Wirt Edwards, II. Georgie, of course, did not have a job, but young Ninian labored as a pressman at his father's place of employment—H.W. Rokker's.[200]

As soon as Albert and Josephine Edwards acquired their complimentary housing, another daughter joined the other two children, Georgie and "Wirt". She was Mary E. (Edwards) Brown, the widow of Charles R. Brown.[201] Since Albert continued as a bookkeeper for Rokker, Mary must have assisted her mother and sister with the chores of housekeeping and guiding the visitors through the open parts of the home.[202] When they first moved in, Albert was 57; Josephine, 55; Georgie, 32; Mary, 30; and "Wirt," as he was known, 29.[203]

Imagine the elation of the Edwardses when Robert Todd

Lincoln rolled into Springfield aboard his private railroad car to participate in the gala events scheduled to observe the centennial of Abraham Lincoln's birth. On February 12, 1909, Robert slipped into the Lincoln home, greeted his kin, and asked to go up to his old bed chamber where he had slept as a boy. "In the sacred presence of memory he was left alone in the room and remained there some time," revealed a reporter, "friends keeping intruders from venturing inside to disturb whatever thought the visit recalled to his mind."

From five until seven p.m. later that evening, the Daughters of the American Revolution held an impressive reception at the Lincoln dwelling with Mrs. A.S., Josephine Edwards, presiding as the hostess. Standing with her in the receiving line was the famed Susan Lawrence Dana, one of the wealthiest women in Springfield. She resided in Lawrence House, (Dana House) built between 1902 and 1904 at the northwest corner of Fourth and Lawrence. It had been designed for her in Prairie Style by none other than Frank Lloyd Wright. For these festivities, Susan had accepted as her houseguest Mrs. Donald McLean, the National President of the D.A.R. who had steamed into Springfield the day before on the Kansas City Hummer.[204]

To commemorate the 50th anniversary of Abraham Lincoln's leaving Springfield to assume the duties of President at Washington, D.C., President William Howard Taft rumbled into Illinois' Capital City at 1:45 p.m. on February 11, 1911. He arrived from Decatur on board the

Illinois Traction System, an electric train. Historians asserted it was the first time that a President had ridden on an electric railway. Robert Lincoln had promised to join Taft in Springfield, but illness forced him to remain in Chicago. Quickly, Pres. Taft presented himself at the Old State House, the Lincoln & Herndon Law Office, and the Lincoln Tomb. Then, shortly before 4 p.m., the President made a pilgrimage to the Lincoln home with Gov. Charles S. Deneen, a fellow Republican, and other State officials. There, he was presented to Mrs. A.S. Edwards who acted as his knowledgeable guide. "I wish to walk upon the floors that Lincoln trod," Taft implored her simply. His request was quickly honored, and Taft became the first President to tour the entire residence of the Lincolns. A local reporter, who followed the Presidential party, remarked with a literary flare that during his brief visit "the sound of a living president's footsteps roused the echoes of one gone before." Just prior to departing, Taft sat down at the priceless desk once used by Lincoln in his old law office and signed his name upon the visitors' register. The chair which held the heavy weight of the huge President happened to be one in which Daniel Webster had once reposed. For some reason, it had become part of the relics collection in the Lincoln home.[205]

Another American hero called at the Lincoln home on April 7, 1912. This was the flamboyant Ex-President Theodore Roosevelt. It would seem that the Edwardses had more than their share of distinguished guests during their tenure of office as custodians. Col. Roosevelt also traveled out to Oak Ridge and paid his respects to the martyred Lincoln's memory.[206]

While dressing in his room at the Lincoln home on December 20, 1915, Albert Edwards suffered a heart attack at 7 a.m. and died. Two days after his death, the funeral was conducted in the famous Lincoln residence at 2:30 p.m. by the Rev. S.H. Bowyer of Central Baptist Church and the Rev. Edward Haughton of St. Paul's Episcopal Church. Burial took place at Oak Ridge Cemetery.[207] Most of the Edwardses were Episcopalians, but Albert did not hold membership there at his demise. Yet he had been baptized in this faith on April 5, 1843.

At the death of Albert Edwards, his widow, Josephine, became the official Custodian of the Lincoln shrine, assisted by her two daughters, Mary Edwards Brown and Georgie H. Edwards, who remained with her. Her son lived there, too, but worked outside the home. During Mrs. Edward's term, an important change took place in the governing of the home. On March 7, 1917, Gov. Frank O. Lowden, a Republican, approved legislation defined as "The Civil Administrative Code." This law, in Paragraph 49, Section 7, took the Lincoln home from the Trustees and placed it under the Department of Public Works and Buildings.[208] A Parks and Memorials Division administered it.

Cancer of the gallbladder and liver caused the death of Josephine Edwards on the morning of October 4, 1918, at the Lincoln home. Her funeral took place there at 3 p.m. on the sixth, the Rev. Edward Haughton officiating. She had been a member of his congregation at St. Paul's Episcopal Cathedral. In death, she joined her husband at Oak Ridge; and her daughter, Mary Edwards Brown, became Custodian.

In her youth, the new Custodian had been known as Mamie E. Edwards and had been born in Springfield on September 20, 1866. On May 4, 1886, she was united in marriage by an Episcopal Rector of St. Paul's, to Charles R. Brown, son of Alexander and Sue C. (Thorton) Brown. The groom was twenty-nine and had been born at Versailles, Kentucky, but at the time of his marriage resided at Brighton, Polk County, Missouri, where he raised stock. It would appear that "Mamie" returned to southwest Missouri with her husband. She bore him a son, Remann A. Brown. Then, at about the time that her father received the post of Custodian at the Lincoln residence, she came back to Springfield and reported that she had been widowed. Finding another woman in town by the name of Mamie E. Brown, she adopted Mary Edwards Brown as her identification.[209]

Her sister, Georgie, a spinster, remained in the Lincoln dwelling to assist Mary Edwards Brown. Georgie had been born in Springfield on July 22, 1864; she died on April 10, 1922, at a hospital in Jacksonville, Illinois, where she had been undergoing treatment for a month.

In 1924, Mrs. Brown resigned as Custodian. She continued to reside in Springfield and did not die until August 27, 1958, at the age of nearly 92. The Rector of the Episcopal Church officiated at her burial. Her son then lived in Leesburg, Florida.[210]

Virginia Stuart Brown, a great-granddaughter of John Todd Stuart (Lincoln's first law partner, and evidently no close relation to Mary Edwards Brown) took over as Custodian on July 1, 1924. Her ancestry is most interesting and well worth telling here. John Todd Stuart married Mary V. Nash, a daughter of Gen. Frank Nash, on October 25, 1837. They had a daughter, Elizabeth Jane Stuart, called "Bettie," who was born in July of 1838. She became the wife of Christopher Columbus Brown on October 20, 1859, and produced a son named Edwards Brown. At twenty-four, Edwards took to wife Gertrude May Dement on June 10, 1886. The Rev. James A. Reed, pastor of the First Presbyterian Church at Springfield, performed the ceremony. Gertrude, born September 20, 1865, was a daughter of Henry Dodge and Mary Field (Williams) Dement and had come to Springfield from Dixon, Illinois, when her father assumed the office of Secretary of State on January 17, 1881. He was a Republican and served two terms. Both the Dements and the Browns worshiped at the Presbyterian Church.

On April 12, 1893, Virginia Stuart Brown was born to Edward and Gertrude Brown. Her father was a real estate agent in Springfield but took his family to South Dakota in 1909. There, he died in 1923. His widow and Virginia returned to Springfield where Miss Brown, a maiden lady, acquired the post of Custodian at the Lincoln home. Her mother, Gertrude Dement Brown, immediately moved in with Virginia and assisted with the housekeeping and the visitors.

Two years after mother and daughter took up their residence at the home, Robert Todd Lincoln succumbed in his sleep on July 26, 1926, at his estate, Hildene, near Manchester, Vermont. Later, his body was transferred to Arlington National Cemetery, just outside Washington, D.C. He is the only one of the Lincoln children not buried in the Lincoln Tomb at Springfield with President and Mrs. Abraham Lincoln. Robert had no strong religious connections, although a Congregational minister preached his funeral.

Gertrude Dement Brown remained at the Lincoln home until her death on November 13, 1945, although her actual demise took place at Memorial Hospital in Springfield. Her father, the Hon. Henry Dodge Dement, had been the son of Col. John and Mary L. (Dodge) Dement and the grandson of General Henry Dodge, the first Governor of Wisconsin Territory. Indeed, Gertrude and Virginia stemmed from a distinguished family.

Virginia Stuart Brown, a talented artist and author, administered the Lincoln home until May 1, 1953, when she retired. At Scottsdale, Arizona, she passed away to her reward on May 17, 1970, and was buried in Phoenix.[211]

Kathleen S. Bradish (June 20, 1886-October 25, 1978), the wife of John H. Bradish, Sr., advanced to Custodian on

May 1, 1953. Lincoln's former abode was in the midst of a restoration project supervised by Richard S. Hagen from the Illinois Department of Conservation, which then administered the property. From evidence provided by archaeological excavations and old photographs, the backyard with its woodshed, privy and carriage house were carefully reconstructed as they had appeared during the Lincolns' ownership. A physical survey of the home itself allowed certain restorations and strengthenings to be accomplished so that visitors might tour both the first and second floors of the shrine. Previously, guest could look at only the front and back parlors, the sitting room and the dining room within the first story.[212] The second floor was thrown open to the public on February 12, 1955.

With the whole house open to "historical pilgrims," it is quite obvious that Mrs. Bradish did not actually live in the Lincoln home as had previous custodians. No, she resided at 1008 1/2 Fayette Avenue, as the city directories disclose. And she proved to be the last of the custodians, per se. Personnel records reveal that she retired on December 1, 1958. She and her husband established a home at Ogunquit, York County, Maine, where he passed away on November 9, 1971. Kathleen lived for another seven years.

With much fanfare, on August 18, 1971, President Richard M. Nixon appeared in Springfield, Illinois, to sign one important piece of legislation. In the Hall of the House of Representatives at the Old State House, Pres. Nixon seated himself at the desk used by President-elect Lincoln to write part of his First Inaugural Address. Atop that historic piece of furniture, he put his name to Public Law 92-127: "An Act To authorize the Secretary of the Interior to establish the Lincoln Home National Historic Site in the State of Illinois, and for other purposes." This law allowed the Secretary of the Interior "to acquire by donation, purchase with donated or appropriated funds, or exchange the property and improvements thereon. . .within the area generally depicted on the map" as the Lincoln Home National Historic Site.[213] At last, the Federal Government had taken the first step in making the Lincoln homestead a National Park.

How well the author recalls that date. He assisted with the security preparations for the President's visit and on that torrid day stood with the Honor Guard of the Illinois State Militia that lined both sides of the south walk leading from the State House. He wore his dress blue wool uniform with the silver eagles of a Colonel gleaming on the shoulder straps. As President Nixon and Governor Richard B. Ogilvie took their exit from the Old Capitol, they walked slowly between our files and took the smart salute of these veteran troops. What a thrill for us to witness this event, so important to the State of Illinois and the future of the Lincoln residence.

Next, the Illinois General Assembly passed Senate Bill No. 1420 transferring the Lincoln home and its contents to the Federal Government. Gov. Ogilvie approved it on July

11, 1972.[214] As directed by law, Henry N. Barkhausen, Director of Conservation, gave a quit-claim deed for this property to the Federal Government on October 2, 1972.[215] Albert W. Banton became the first Superintendent of the Lincoln Home National Historic Site on October 9 that year.[216] He immediately commenced to restore and improve the area. A building for the orientation of visitors was planned, as were parking areas, etc.

President Gerald R. Ford flew into Springfield on March 5, 1976, to dedicate the cornerstone already prepared for the Lincoln Home Visitors' Center. First, he spoke to a large crowd assembled in front of the Lincoln home itself, becoming the first President to address a gathering at this hallowed shrine. He informed his chilly listeners that he had previously been at this spot in 1965 but that this was his first visit as President. "I can tell you," explained Ford, "that the presence of Abraham Lincoln is surely there in the White House. . . ." However, he vouched that he had not seen Father Abraham's ghost as others had. Yet he felt Lincoln's great influence every day.

Pres. Ford then proceeded to unveil the red granite cornerstone from Wausau, Wisconsin. Congressman Paul Findley and Supt. Banton assisted him in this colorful ceremony. When the stone came into view, the curious throng of onlookers could see that its lettering read: "It is to Abraham Lincoln that we owe the opportunity to observe our National Bicentennial at peace among ourselves and with all nations. Gerald R. Ford. President of the United States. March 5, 1976."[217]

Again, this author participated in that memorable event and can relate with authority that the day turned out to be almost as cold as the weather had been hot back on August 18, 1971, when Pres. Nixon honored the City of Springfield. This time, however, the author warmed his tall body under the warmth of a military greatcoat which covered his dress blues. With understandable pride, he stood at attention with the Honor Guard, sword in hand, and gave the salute for the entire detail, because he now commanded the Militia with the coveted rank of Major General.

Congressman Findley continued to labor diligently on behalf of the Lincoln home. He managed to secure several pieces of the original furniture owned by the Lincolns. Carefully, Congressman Findley, Al Banton and this author (in several trips) physically carried the loveseat, sofa and two chairs into the Lincoln house and placed them where they had stood so many years ago.[218] How fortunate were we to participate in the making of history which would benefit the countless tourists yet to come after us.

Upon the retirement of Al Banton, a most competent administrator—James T. O'Toole—replaced him on June 23, 1982. He has striven to get the community involved in the Lincoln Home Area and to support his many educational projects and programs. Never should we forget these two fine gentlemen who have supervised Illinois' only National Park.

With this chapter, the saga of the Lincoln home is completed up to the 175th anniversary of Lincoln's birth. This wonderful old structure has witnessed unexcelled joy, as when an official committee called in person on May 19, 1860, to inform the "Railsplitter" that he had received the Republican nomination for President. And it has seen unspeakable grief, as when Edward Baker Lincoln died there February 1, 1850. It has also heard the childish shrieks of laughter, as when Mrs. Lincoln invited Willie's playmates for a Holiday party at 3 p.m. on December 23, 1857. For these and many other reasons, the Lincoln home receives thousands of visitors each year. It is one of the most popular shrines in the entire world. May it stand forever to remind us of the incomparable Abraham Lincoln who wanted freedom for every man.

References

186 *Illinois State Register*, Oct. 8, 1922, p. 1, cc. 4-5; Death Record, Dept. of Public Health; Adj. Gen. Files, MSS., Illinois State Archives.

187 Marriage Licenses, IV, No. 1577, MS., County Bldg.,

Springfield, Ill.; *Springfield City Directory For 1866,* 21*; U.S. Census 1880*, Springfield, Sangamon Co., Ill., E.D. 229, p. 18, 1. 20; Death Record, Dept. of Public Health.

188 *Springfield City Directory 1877-78*, 52.

189 Election Returns: County Officers, 1882-1905, 193; Commission Records of County Officers, 1873-1929, 247, MSS., Illinois State Archives.

190 *Springfield City Directory 1894*, 239.

191 *Reports to the General Assembly of Illinois 1894*, X, No. 12, pp. 1-5; *Biennial Report of the Secretary of State* (Springfield: Phillips Bros., 1897), 186-187.

192 *Jour. Ill. State Hist. Soc.*, LXXIV, 296; John S. Goff, *Robert Todd Lincoln* (Norman: Univ. of Oklahoma Press, 1969), 259.

193 Five items concerning the Edwards appointment in SC 923, MSS., Illinois State Hist. Lib.

194 *The Illinois State Journal*, June 30, 1897, p. 6, c. 2.

195 *Springfield City Directory 1898* (Springfield: R.L. Polk & Co., 1898), 271.

196 Death Record, Dept. of Public Health.

197 *Ibid.*; *Illinois State Register*, Oct. 8, 1922, p. 1, cc. 4-5.

198 Auditor's Receipt Book, XXXIV, 784; XXXV, 106, MSS., Illinois State Archives.

199 Death Records, Dept. of Public Health; Power, *History of Sangamon Co.*, 278-279.

200 *Springfield City Directory 1896*, 131, 132, 405. At this time, the City of Springfield had a population of 42,987.

201 *Ibid.*, 1898, 101.

202 *Ibid.*, 1900, 179.

203 U.S. Census 1880, Springfield, Sangamon Co., Ill., E.D. 230, p. 12, 11. 1-6.

204 *Illinois State Journal*, Feb. 12, 1909, p. 1, cc. 6-7, p. 2, c. 6; Feb. 13, 1909, p. 3, c. 4. Dana House (Lawrence home) is now owned by the State of Illinois and is open for tours.

205 *Ibid.* Feb. 12, 1911, p. 1, c. 1; p. 2, c. 1; p. 4, cc. 3-4. Local Masons especially enjoyed Taft's visit, because he had been made a member of the Craft on Feb. 18, 1909, by the Grand Master of Ohio. Gov. Deneen was also a Mason.

206 *Ibid.*, Apr. 8, 1912, p. 2, c. 2.

207 *Ibid.*, Dec. 21, 1915, p. 7, c. 1; Dec. 22, 1915, p. 7, c. 1; Death Record, XII, 347, Sangamon Co. Clerk's Office, Springfield, Ill.

208 *Laws of the State of Illinois Enacted by the Fiftieth General Assembly* (Springfield: Ill. State Journal Co., 1917), 2-36. Gov. Lowden was also a Mason.

209 *Illinois State Journal*, Oct. 5, 1918, p. 7, c. 7; Death Record, Dept. of Public Health; Register of Marriages, B, 30, Sangamon Co. Bldg.; *Illinois State Journal*, Aug. 28, 1958, p. 1, cc. 2-3.

210 Death Records, Dept. of Public Health. Ninian Wirt Edwards, II, died May 19, 1942, at his residence, 313 W. Cook in Springfield. He was a retired pressman and had been born June 30, 1868. *Illinois State Register*, May 20, 1942, p. 5, c. 3.

211 *Illinois State Journal*, Nov. 14, 1945, p. 10, c. 3; May 18, 1970, p. 4, c. 2; Register of Marriages, B, 34.

212 *Jour. Ill. State Hist. Soc.*, XLVIII, 5-27.

213 *U.S. Statutes at Large* (Washington: Govt. Print. Office, 1972), LXXXV, 347.

214 *Laws of the State of Illinois Passed by the Seventy-Seventh General Assembly*, I, 501-502. Gov. Ogilvie is a member of the Craft, too.

215 Deed Record, Vol. 656, pp. 1-3, Sangamon Co. Bldg.

216 Banton is not only a Freemason but also a Past Master.

217 *The State Journal-Register*, Mar. 6, 1976, p. 1, cc. 1-4; p. 9, cc. 1-6. Pres. Ford is a Freemason and in this ceremony was doing what Masons are known for doing: laying cornerstones.

218 Notes kept by the author at the time the furniture was returned to the Lincoln home.

Mary Lincoln baked her noted "white cake" for her husband who had just been elected President. Drawing by Lloyd Ostendorf

Appendix I

Personal Habits and Manners of President Lincoln

A correspondent of the *Utica Herald* gives the following as the reminiscences of a Mr. Eaton, of Springfield, who said he knew Mr. Lincoln for 30 years:[1]

> I am a carpenter, and built his house for him.[2] He was often in my house and I in his. I sold him the first and I think the only cow he ever owned. He came for her himself and led her home with a rope. He was the most common, sociable man I ever knew. His wife was rather quick-tempered, used to fret and scold about a great deal, but I don't believe Mr. Lincoln was ever angry in his life.[3] I knew him when he first came to Springfield.[4] There were only a few scattered houses when I came. Young Lincoln, I remember, was an awkward, hard-working young man. Everybody said he would never make a good

lawyer, because he was too honest. He came to my shop one day, after I had been here five or six months, and said he had a notion to quit studying law and learn the carpenter's trade. He thought there was more need of carpenters than lawyers.[5]

Mrs. Lincoln's folks were dreadfully opposed to her union with Abe.[6] She had two sisters and a [cousin] living here;[7] they live here now, and are very wealthy, aristocratic and highly respectable people. Mrs. Lincoln never goes there; they have never spoken to each other as I know of since the day she and Lincoln were married.[8] They would not speak to her because she had brought such disgrace upon them by marrying Abe Lincoln. After Lincoln began to show his colors a little, began to be popular, Mrs. Lincoln would not speak to them, but Abe was on good terms with everybody.

He used always to do his own marketing, even after he was elected President, and before he went to Washington I used to see him at the baker's and butcher's every morning with his basket on his arm. Everybody respected him—no more after he was President than they did before. He was kind and sociable with every one. He would speak to every one. After he was elected we would sometimes address him as "Mr. President," or, "glad to shake the hand of our President." "Well, yes, I suppose so," he would say. "I shall have to go and leave you before long. You must call and see me when I am living in the big house." He was so common, so kind, so childlike, that I don't believe there was one in this city but who loved him as a father or brother.

He was a very liberal man, too much so, perhaps, for his own good. I am one of the trustees of the First Baptist Church,[9] and although Mr. Lincoln was not an attendant with our congregation, he would always give $15, $20 or $25 every year to help support the minister. He was sure to give something to every charitable and benevolent purpose that came along. "Well, how much do you want that I should give?" he would say, drawing his purse. "You must leave me a little to feed the babies with."

There was considerable talk here about Mrs. Lincoln's bad temper. She was very irritable, and would often say things she would afterward be sorry for. I have often heard her say to Mr. Lincoln, "Why don't you dress up and try to look like somebody?" Sometimes she would get in a stew and refuse to get his meals for him. I was one morning in the eating saloon round on Monroe street fixing up a counter, when Mr. Lincoln and his oldest son, Robert, then only a little boy, came in and ordered breakfast. After the meal was served, Mr. Lincoln, leaning back in his chair and commencing to pick his teeth, says to the boy, who had not quite finished, "Well, Robby, this ain't so very bad after all, is it? If ma don't conclude to let us come back we will board here all summer."

He never seemed to be the least ruffled—always calm and pleasant. Lincoln was sitting in the telegraph office talking with everybody around him as usual, when the dispatch came announcing his nomination to the Presidency by the Chicago Convention.[10] After the dispatch was read, Mr. Lincoln got up and said, "There is a woman over to my house who I guess would be pleased to hear that bit of news. I'll walk over and tell it to her." He was never cast down by adversity, never elated by success.

References for Appendix I

1 Reprinted in the Belvidere (Ill.) *Standard*, Tuesday, Apr. 14, 1868, p. 1.

2 Page Eaton, as we now know, worked with his father, John Eaton, Jr., on this construction project.

3 Like most people, Abraham Lincoln did find things that vexed him, but he generally held his temper very well.

4 Lincoln rode into Springfield on April 15, 1837. Page Eaton did not come to town until May of 1839. Perhaps the newspaper reporter confused several of the statements made to him by Eaton.

5 Lincoln may have been merely making conversation with the Eatons. Yet we do know that young Lincoln at New Salem contemplated becoming a blacksmith. He himself revealed this thought in 1860. Basler, ed., *The Collected Works*, IV, 65. Thomas Lincoln, his father, was an excellent carpenter, and Abraham Lincoln had built flatboats, etc.

6 This opinion is greatly exaggerated. Mary's father liked Lincoln very much.

7 Frances Jane (Todd) Wallace; Elizabeth Porter (Todd) Edwards; and John Todd Stuart. Ann Maria (Todd) Smith also came after Mary did.

8 Another greatly exaggerated statement.

9 This is another example of the poor reporting done by the journalist who interviewed Page Eaton. Eaton was certainly a member of the First Methodist Episcopal Church, Capitol and Fifth streets, since a minister from this church buried him and his wife. Although early records are not extant for this Methodist Church, later ones show mem-

bers of his family as members. Membership records are available for the Baptist Church for this period, and they do not show Page Eaton.

10 On May 18, 1860. The telegraph office stood on the North side of the Public Square and had the only wires into the city at that time.

Appendix II

Marinette Co. Man Personally Knew Lincoln

Knud Olsen, A Pioneer of Middle Inlet, Recalls Incidents In Career Of Martyred President[1]

Knud Olsen, residing near Middle Inlet, [Wisconsin] relates interesting incidents in the life of President Abraham Lincoln and also some of his own unique experiences. He is probably the only man in Marinette County who the martyred president actually saw and talked with. In a letter received in reply to a request, Mr. Olsen writes as follows:

> I was born in Norway Nov. 10, 1838, worked at the miller trade up to the time I left there in 1858; landed at a quarantine hospital in Del. I had caught the yellow fever from Cuba. I had worked my way from Scotland and landed at Cuba. I was mistreated quite a little on the way, as I did not understand the

commands of the officers.

In 1858 and '59 I worked in carriage and blacksmith work for $4.00 per month. Left Penn in '59 and landed in Springfield, Ill., and worked at carpenter work for Mr. John Armstrong, who was a particular friend of Mr. Lincoln and that is how I came to know Mr. Lincoln as I was sent there to work and got to know the Lincoln family. In 1861 I was married to Miss Bertha Lund and lived in Springfield till 1870.

Lincoln Campaign

Mr. Armstrong, who I learned my trade by[,] was a delegate to the Republican Convention to Chicago[2] and when he came home I heard him tell how Lincoln came to be nominated as Republican President. He said that Lincoln came in as the black horse. In 1860 on August 8th there was the greatest demonstration at Springfield there ever was for any President.[3] I guess there were delegates from every part of the state. There were a good many bands and they had had a great many floats out, one in particular was a big log drawn by a number of oxen on a wagon and a man splitting rails. There was a larger crowd at that demonstration than there was when the men were called to arms in the time of the war. I stood on a stone pile with one of my fellow workmen who worked for Mr. Armstrong. He was a Douglas man and I was a Lincoln man. We were hollering in each other's face. When I hollered for Lincoln he would holler for Douglas. Then I would holler take a rope and hang him and he'd come right back at me. At that time, I was a strong Republican and I hollered myself hoarse and if there was a Republican like Lincoln in the field today I would vote the Republican ticket, but there is as much difference between the Republican now and then as there is between night and day. I had the pleasure of shaking hands with Mr. Lincoln after he was elected President. He stood at the capitol all day receiving congratulations. One of my friends asked Mr. Lincoln, while shaking hands, what he thought of the times as there was [a] great deal of trouble in the country and he answered him that he thought it would be all straightened out without trouble when he got to Washington. He did not profess to be a Christian, but his work brought him nearer to being a Christian than most Christians of today. In Lincoln's speech at Gettysburg, Penn. he said with "malice towards none and charity to all, let us pursue the right as God lets us see the right," which was plainly demonstrated in his pursuit in life. This was shortly before his assassination.[4]

After the Assassination

At the time he was assassinated I stood on the depot platform at Macon, Ill., when the news came there and I saw a man by the name of Ellis come running out and after him came old Uncle Bobby, as they called him, an old farmer. Ellis, when he heard the news, said I only hope to God it is time [true] that he is killed and old Uncle Bob, who sat playing cards, grabbed up his blacksnake which lay under the table and struck Ellis with it and took after him down the street. Ellis skipped to Taylorville, Christian County, Ill., where they were mostly rebel sympathizers as himself and he never came back to Macon from that day till this as far as I knew.

My wife stood in the crowd at Springfield for about four hours while waiting to see his remains before she got to see him.[5] I never saw his remains after he was dead.

In 1867 the man I worked for had the blueprint for Lincoln's monument and he set a German man named Wagner and me to work making a model which was sent to Vermont to have the stones cut after for the monument. This is all I can recollect of Lincoln at the present time.

I left Springfield in 1870 with my wife and five children and settled at Green Bay, Brown County,

Wis. Lived on a farm at [New] Denmark, Wis., till 1879 when I moved to Middle Inlet, Wis., where I have resided since. I am a man 82 years of age now and enjoy my fishing trips as well as any man of today though I do get tired from a long walk in the heat and fighting mosquitoes.

Sell Lincoln Rails

A news agent at Springfield went out and bought up all the rails around where Lincoln split rails and sold them in small pieces for a dollar a piece from which people made canes, picture frames or other small articles to remember Lincoln by.

Respectfully,
Knud Olsen

References

1 Marinette (Wis.) *Eagle-Star*, June 14, 1920, p. 2, cc. 3-4.

2 John Armstrong was not listed as a voting delegate but no doubt attended the nominating convention on a special pass. He worked actively for A. Lincoln's election.

3 Olsen has exactly the correct date for this event, proving that he must have saved a clipping from the local newspaper.

4 Here, Olsen confuses Lincoln's Second Inaugural Address of March 4, 1865, with his Gettysburg Address of November 19, 1863. In the former, Lincoln said, "With malice toward none; with charity for all; with firmness in the right, as God gives us o see the right, let us strive on to finish the work we are in; to bind up the nation's wounds; to care for him who shall have borne the battle, and for his widow, and his orphan—to do all which may achieve and cherish a just, and a lasting peace, among ourselves, and with all nations."

5 On May 3-4, 1865, Pres. Lincoln's remains were placed on view in the House of Representatives at the Capitol on the Public Square in Springfield, Illinois.

Appendix III

Two More Funerals in the Lincoln Home

Shortly after the Albert Stevenson Edwardses moved into the old Lincoln residence on July 1, 1897, they offered their home for a private family funeral observance. Albert's sister, Julia Cook Edwards, who was born in Springfield on April 29, 1837, the daughter of Elizabeth Porter (Todd) and Ninian Wirt Edwards, had married Edward Lewis Baker, Sr., on June 6, 1855. Baker—born on June 3, 1829, had graduated from Shurtleff College and studied law at Harvard. Later, he acquired half interest in the *Illinois State Journal* at Springfield. Eventually, he was appointed United States Consul to Buenos Aires in Argentina on December 8, 1873. He left town for his station in South America during March of 1874.[1]

On June 21, 1897, Consul Baker was involved in an accident which resulted in his death on July 8 that year.[2] His body was shipped back to Springfield where it arrived by train at 6:57 a.m. on August 25 and was immediately transported to the Lincoln home where Albert Edwards served as the custodian for the State of Illinois. The immediate family of the deceased took temporary lodgings with the Edwardses while family and friends called to pay their respects until the casket was taken to the First Presbyterian Church on the following day. There, at 10 a.m. the Rev. Frederick H. Wines, a former pastor of this congregation, conducted the funeral service. Burial followed at Oak Ridge Cemetery.[3]

When E.L. Baker's widow, Mrs. Julia Cook (Edwards) Baker, died at midnight in Chicago on July 29, 1908, the corpse was sent by train down to Springfield. The coffin arrived during the morning of July 31 and was unloaded and taken to the Lincoln home where the Albert Edwardses still presided as caretakers. That afternoon at 2:30, the Rev. F.A. DeRosset of St. Paul's Episcopal Church preached her funeral obsequies. At the conclusion of these ceremonies, the casket was conducted out to Oak Ridge Cemetery and buried.[4]

References

1 John Carroll Power, *History of the Early Settlers of Sangamon County, Illinois* (Springfield: Edwin A. Wilson & Co., 1876), 278; *Illinois State Journal*, Mar. 25, 1874, p. 4 c. 1.

2 *Illinois State Journal*, July 10, 1897, p. 6, c. 3.

3 *Ibid.*, Aug. 25, 1897, p. 5, c. 2, Aug. 26, 1897, p. 6, cc. 4-5.

4 *Ibid.*, July 31, 1908, p. 6, c. 4, Aug. 1, 1908, p. 6, c. 4.

T. D. Jones' bust of Lincoln. Jones modeled this from life in the St. Nicholas Hotel, Springfield, Illinois, during parts of 1860-1861.

Feb. 20, 1970 photo by "Doc" Helm

Appendix IV

Two Female Lodgers

Although later Springfield directories listed residents by street address, one official custodian of the Lincoln Home—Virginia Stuart Brown— "neglected" to inform the compilers of the directories that other than family members resided with her at times. Fortunately, friends[1] have now informed the author of two single ladies who once had living quarters in the Lincoln Home. A check of the alphabetical listings in the directories quickly revealed that this valuable information was entirely correct. Both of these ladies were at times listed as living at 430 South Eight Street, the address of the Lincoln Home.

Until February 12, 1955, the second floor of the Lincoln Home remained closed to the public, but served as private living quarters of the custodians. So, it was possible for a caretaker to permit others to occupy unused rooms on the upper level as well as make use of the kitchen on the first floor.

The first known "outsider" to dwell with Miss Brown was Miss Margaret Luella Stiles, daughter of Jay Perry and Bessie Arvilla (Saxton) Stiles. She was born on July 4, 1915. At the time of her birth, her parents were farmers and lived near the village of Steward in Alto Township of Lee County, Illinois. Her father had been reared there, but her mother stemmed from Central City in Nebraska.However, the Stiles family later moved to Savanna on the Mississippi River in Carrol County, Illinois.[2] There, Margaret graduated from high school. After receiving a business education, she eventually found a position in Springfield, Illinois, where she had relatives and friends.

At the age of twenty, in 1935, Miss Stiles took up living quarters at 414 East Canedy Street. She worked as a stenographer for the Herman Pierik Trust which had its offices in the Ridgely Farmers Bank Building on the southeast corner of Fifth and Monroe.[3] But the following year she became the stenographer for the Disabled American Veterans of the World War, Department of Illinois, which operated out of 407-409 in the Ferguson Building at the southwest corner of Sixth and Monroe. Her residence remained the same.[4]

In 1937, Margaret advanced to be the personal secretary and stenographer for Albert H. Sonius, the Adjutant for the Disabled American Veterans. Although her office was in the same building, her residence suddenly changed to 430 South Eight Street, the Lincoln Home.[5] It is thought that she had become acquainted with prominent citizens of

Springfield who introduced her to Virginia Stuart Brown.

It is quite doubtful that Miss Brown charged Miss Stiles rent. The official custodian probably enjoyed the companionship of her new roomer who undoubtedly also assisted with the housework and perhaps at times with the custodian's aged mother, Gertrude (Dement) Brown. We know Margaret Stiles slept in the so-called "maid's room." She was allowed to use the kitchen, the telephone and to entertain gentlemen callers. Miss Brown would cordially mix cocktails for those who came to visit Miss Stiles. It proved to be a most agreeable arrangement.[6]

Miss Stiles was a most beautiful woman, and it was not long until eligible bachelors began to call upon her. Charles J. Northrup, an attorney, paid her court and recalls drinking cocktails in the kitchen with her. However, it was a handsome young officer who next courted her very seriously. This was Clifford Murray Hathaway, Jr., a Captain in the Ordnance Department of th United States Army. He would ring the doorbell at the Lincoln Home in the evenings and then be let into the house by the rear entrance. An icy mixed drink and conversation awaited him in the kitchen. When he was called to active duty, he then directed love letters to her at the Lincoln Home where she continued to reside. These he still has in his possession.

Miss Stiles changed positions in 1938, becoming a stenographer for the Family Welfare Association at 615 East Jefferson Street. There, she met such outstanding

Springfield citizens as Pascal E. Hatch and others.[7] She continued with this employment but became their bookkeeper in 1942, the last year that she worked for this agency.[8] On November 14, 1942, she married her most ardent suitor, Captain Hathaway, and left the historic Lincoln Home.[9] The young couple established their residence at 829 South State Street, but the husband was away fighting a war in Europe for some time after his marriage.[10]

Mrs. Hathaway died in Springfield on January 22, 1978, as a result of cancer. She was survived by her husband, Colonel Hathaway, and two sons, Clifford M. Hathaway, III, and John J. Hathaway. Her funeral service was held on January 25 in the church where she held membership, Christ Episcopal—just two blocks west of the house where the Lincolns and she also had once lived—with burial in Camp Butler National Cemetery. She had also been a member of Philanthropic Educational Organization, a sisterhood, as well as other groups.[11] Mrs. Hathaway had experienced a most interesting and useful life. Only a handful of people could boast that they had actually resided for five years in the famous Lincoln Home and felt all about themselves the unseen influence and force of the Lincoln legend.

The next house guest of Virginia Stuart Brown in the Lincoln Home was Miss Ester Sophia Duncan, the very talented daughter of Richard Yates and Carrie (Reinbach) Duncan. She had been born in Franklin, Morgan County, Illinois, on July 8, 1900.[12] Her parents had taken their marriage vows in Franklin on May 1, 1884. Her father had been born in Jacksonville on February 20, 1860; her mother, April 2, 1862, in Franklin. The Reinbachs had come from Germany in 1849, and Carrie's father earned his living as a merchant in Franklin.

Richard Yates Duncan was the son of John Blankenship and Adeline G. (Wright) Duncan who were married March 21, 1844. John had been born in Tennessee on August 10, 1817, but removed to Morgan County as a young man where he practiced law and became a judge. Miss Wright had been born in Frankfort, Kentucky, June 17, 1823, but her parents relocated to Illinois during 1829. When the Mexican War broke out, John enlisted as First Sergeant of Company G in the First Illinois Infantry Regiment. In the Civil War, he served as Captain of Company H, 32nd Infantry Regiment, Illinois Volunteers. Unfortunately, he was severely wounded while in Tennessee and died soon afterward, in 1864.

Having been bereft of his father at the age of four, Richard Yates Duncan had little opportunity to follow the law, as his father had done, but rather learned the blacksmith's trade as did two of his brothers. He had only a common school education yet was respected in his community because of his sound judgement and common sense. He became a town trustee. When Ester Duncan was born, he was still engaged in blacksmithing at Franklin.[13] However, the Duncans later moved to Maple Street in Mount Sterling,

Brown County, where Richard continued to operate his own blacksmith shop.[14] Esther attended high school in Mount Sterling from 1915 until she graduated in 1919. Then, in 1926, she received a Bachelor of Music Degree in piano.[15] Evidently, she worked as an instructor during some of her undergraduate years at Illinois College. That would account for her taking six years to graduate.

After teaching music at Roodhouse and Mount Sterling, Miss Duncan in 1939, accepted a position as music teacher at Lanphier High School in Springfield.[16] Upon coming to the Capital City, she was invited by Miss Virginia Stuart Brown to live with her in the Lincoln Home. She took up residence that same year with Miss Brown, joining Miss Stiles who had already been at 430 South Eight Street for two years.[17] Observers would have noted that Miss Duncan was then thirty-nine years of age, quite short and rather chubby with very small hands and feet. She had been blessed with a natural musical ability which had been honed to perfection by arduous training and practice. At Lanphier High School, located on North Grand Avenue near Eleventh Street, she conducted classes in vocal music which was now her special teaching field. With extraordinary skill, Miss Duncan could extract the very best performances from her musical charges. And yet, her students admired her greatly and strove to achieve her every demand. Since she possessed an ear which could detect perfect pitch, she also directed the a capella choir. One of the former students,

Catherine Lavin Locher, testified that Miss Duncan had inspired her enormously after she "was lucky enough to get in the Lanphier A Capella choir" under her leadership. Of all her old teachers, this one stood out in her memory more than any other.[18]

Although Miss Stiles married in November of 1942 and left the Lincoln Home, Miss Duncan remained there with Miss Brown and her mother. But during the summer vacation months of 1944, 1945, 1946 and 1947, Miss Duncan left to attend graduate classes at the Teachers College of Columbia University in New York City. She obtained her Master of Arts degree from that institution on December 17, 1947, with a major in Music and Music Education.[19]

After Mrs. Gertrude (Dement) Brown died on November 13, 1945, Miss Duncan was evidently the only companion of Virginia Stuart Brown in the Lincoln Home. None other has been discovered in a careful search of the city directories.[20] Miss Duncan remained in the Lincoln Home until about 1950. By this time, she had removed to 2038 South Lincoln.[21] She continued to teach music at Lanphier High School, but in 1953 she announced that she had also become the Director of Music at the First Christian Church on the southeast corner of Sixth and Cook streets in Springfield. She was a member of this denomination, as had been her mother.[22]

Although Esther remained at Lanphier as an instructor, by 1965 she had established her residence at 824 Grove

Street in Jacksonville.[23] And the following year she resigned from school teaching. However, she continued to commute back and forth to Springfield in order to give private lessons in piano and voice. Finally, in 1979, she completely retired from her profession.

At the age of 92, on July 19, 1992, Miss Duncan passed away at the Barton W. Stone Christian Home in Jacksonville. Congestive heart failure caused her demise. She had never been married. Rather , she gave all her attention to her career in music.It had been a successful career. She became the first president of the Illinois Music Educator's Association and was a member of the National Music Education Conference. At one time she also served as president of the Altrusa Club. In addition, she was given the Valley Forge Freedom Foundation Teacher's Award.

After a burial service at the Gillham-Buchanan Funeral home in Jacksonville, her body was interred at the Franklin Cemetery at Franklin, Illinois, her old home town.[24]

References

1 Charles J. Northrup, Col. Clifford Murray Hathaway, Jr., and Patricia Ann (Pile) Hauversburk.

2 Delayed Birth Certificate No. 6535, MS., Illinois Dept. of Public Health: Vital Records, Springfield, Ill.

3 *Directory of Springfield, Illinois 1935* (Springfield: A.L. Williamson, 1935), 855, 713.

4 *Ibid.*, 1936 (Springfield: H.L. Williamson, 1936), 879, 307.

5 *Ibid.*, 1937 (Springfield: Williamson Printing & Publishing Co., 1937), 1190, 1181, 900.

6 Personal Interview with Col. Clifford M. Hathaway, Springfield, Illinois, Oct. 6, 1994, and Charles J. Northrup, Springfield, Illinois, Nov. 27, 1995.

7 *Springfield City Directory 1938* (Springfield: Williamson Printing Co., 1938), 380, 120.

8 *Ibid.*, 1942-43 (Springfield: Storm Directory Co., 1942), 810, 254.

9 *Illinois State Register*, Nov. 10, 1942, p. 7, c. 3.

10 *Springfield City Directory 1944* (Springfield: Storm Directory Co., 1944), 472.

11 Death Record No. 78 004316, MS., Ill. Dept. of Public Health: Vital Records, Springfield, Ill.; *The State Journal-Register*, Jan 23, 1978, p. 17, c. 5 (afternoon edition).

12 Delayed Certificate of Birth, No. 22345, MS., Ill. Dept. of Public Health: Vital Records. The only document found that lists her middle name is her student record at Illinois College.

13 *Portrait and Biographical Album of Morgan and Scott Counties, Ills.* (Chicago: Chapman Bros., 1889), 283-284; *Family History of Morgan County* (Jacksonville: Privately printed, 1976), 90; Delayed Certificate of Birth, No. 22345.

14 U.S. Census 1920,Mount Sterling, Brown Co., Illinois, Vol. 9, ED 7, Sheet 9, Line 66.

15 Miss Duncan's school record in the Registrar's Office, Illinois College, Jacksonville.

16 *The State Journal-Register*, July 21, 1992, p. 7, c. 1.

17. *Springfield. . .1939 Directory* (Springfield: Williamson Printing Co., 1939), 98.

18 Recollections of Patricia A. (Pile) Hauversburk and Janet Bruns; *Lan Hi Yearbook 1950*, 77; *The State Journal-Register*, July 29, 1992, p. 4, c. 5.

19 School Record of Miss Duncan from the Office of the Registrar, Teachers College Columbia University, courtesy of Consuelo Campos, Sept. 29, 1994.

20 *Springfield City Directory 1946-47* (Springfield: H.L. Williamson & Co., 1946), 397, 229.

21 *Polk's Springfield City Directory 1951* (Springfield: R.L. Polk & Co., 1952), 160.

22 *Ibid., 1953* (Springfield: R.L. Polk & Co., 1954), 193; *Portrait and Biographical Album of Morgan and Scott Counties, Ills.*, 284.

23 *Ibid., 1965* (Springfield: R.L. Polk & Co., 1965), 201.

24. *The State Journal-Register*, July 21, 1992,p. 7, c. 1; Death Record No. 92 040126, MS., Ill. Dept. of Public Health: Vital Records, Springfield, Ill.

$5.00

July 28. 1860

Springfield Marine & Fire Ins. Co.

Please pay Mrs Barbara Dinkel

Five dollars in currency

A. Lincoln

Hand-written check by Abraham Lincoln to Mrs. Barbara Dinkel for the sum of \$5.00 was offered on eBay in 2000. It was drawn on the "Springfield Marine and Fire Ins. Co." and is dated July 28, 1860. At that time, the Republican National Convention (in Chicago) had already named Lincoln as its choice for president. This autographed document is accompanied by a Christie's Auction (New York, NY) letter provenance.

Appendix V

New Light on the Lincoln Home Expansion

During the recent restoration of the Lincoln home in Springfield, Illinois, employees of the National Park Service discovered that the expansion of this historic shrine had taken place over a longer period of time than previously though. Until then, research historians had been mostly limited to a contemporary letter written by Mrs. John Todd Stuart to her daughter on April 3, 1856, which reported that "Mr Lincoln has commenced raising his back building two stories high," and a local, 1857, newspaper account showing the cost of this construction project.[1] But it stands to reason that the Lincolns would have commenced the expansion or remodeling of their story-and-a-half house with that front portion facing Eighth Street.

There do exist, nevertheless, several old manuscript sources which tend to support vaguely that some remodeling began on the Lincoln lot prior to 1856. First, Abraham

Lincoln, on June 11, 1850, asked Nathaniel Hay to furnish bricks to build a foundation for a wooden fence to be erected for fifty feet along the west side of his property. (This was the length of his frontage on Eighth Street.) He directed that the footing be of proper width and depth and rise two feet above the soil.[2] Such a wall would also retain the dirt bank protecting the foundations of the house and also help to prevent water from running into the basement which existed only under the front section of the home.

Five years later, court records reveal that on June 4, 1855, Abraham Lincoln purchased an additional 2000 bricks from Nathaniel Hay (for $16) to be used in a foundation for a fence along the Jackson Street side of his residence. This structure would match the front wall as well as its fence and complete the embankment project of stabilization and beautification. Again, in August of that same year, he acquired more bricks from Hay to fabricate a privy vault behind the house.[3]

In addition, a member of the Todd family disclosed that sometime after December of 1854, there had been a fire in the Lincoln home.[4] Thus, here was another reason, or excuse, to continue the remodeling and upgrading of the Lincoln house.

Mary (Todd) Lincoln, on September 18, 1854, sold eighty acres of farm land which her father, Robert Smith Todd, had given her back in 1844. She received $1200 for it from Robert Anderson. A Springfield newspaper revealed that the enlargement of the Lincoln residence cost $1300, just one hundred dollars more than Mary had realized from the sale of her real estate. So, she alone had nearly enough cash on hand to pay for the expansion just shortly before the extensive carpentry work was initiated the following spring. It might be argued very strongly that she sold the land in order to hire the building contractors. Being headstrong and sometimes willful, perhaps Mary did engage the builders without her husband's knowledge. The answer to that question will probably never be discovered.

Now here is a new primary source which declares that there was a major expansion of the Lincoln residence in *1855*. This enlightening interview was published on April 5, 1893, in the *Sangamo Monitor* of Springfield, Illinois. So, why has no previous Lincoln scholar utilized such vital information? Because there is no extant file of that newspaper for this date. Most fortunately, though, Luann Elvey, of East Tawas, Michigan, has a clearly identified clipping of this exact date from this very newspaper. It reveals a tale told by her direct ancestor, John A. Sylvester, an immigrant Portuguese carpenter from Madeira who labored on the enlargement of the Lincoln residence. This precious slip of old newsprint has passed down through her family line and now rests in her loving hands, together with one of the walnut boxes mentioned in the newspaper interview. Luann Elvey's mother is Annajean (Sherman) Elvey. The latter's mother was Rhea Mildred

(Sylvester) Sherman whose father was John O. Sylvester. His father was John A. Sylvester.[5] Here is the interview:

The Sylvester interview
A Lincoln Memorial With a Most Interesting History—
The Handiwork of a Springfield Mechanic.

Our old friend, John A. Sylvester—than whom among mechanics few better could be found a few years ago, when in his more vigorous days—has just finished and placed with Mrs. Charles Ridgely,[6] to be sent to the World's Fair,[7] a beautiful walnut box, inlaid with 1,219 pieces of wood, comprising four or five varieties, which is surrounded with quite a history. In 1855, Mrs. Lincoln decided that she wanted another story on the one-story house the family then occupied. She had fixed upon a time when Mr. Lincoln would be out on the circuit to have the work done, and had engaged Messrs. Hann[on] & Ragsdale, the leading carpenters at that time, to do the work.[8] Mr. Lincoln would be on the circuit about six weeks, and the firm had agreed to complete the work before his return.[9] The house was completed and everything so thoroughly transmogrified, that it is said Mr. Lincoln, when he returned, did not recognize the place, and was standing on the street looking around somewhat amazed, when he saw Mr. Abner Wilkinson, a tailor (still alive and residing at LaCross, Wis.) living on the opposite side of Eighth street, when he called out, "Wilkie can you tell me where old Abe

Lincoln lived around these parts?"[10] He was astonished to see what had been done and remarked to his wife when she met him, "Well, Mary, you remind me of the story of the fellow who went to California and left one ba[b]y at home and when he returned three years after, found three. The fellow looked at his wife and then at the children and said, "Well, Lizzie, for a little woman and without help, you have raised thunder amazingly." He [Lincoln] was delighted with the change and always referred to it as an evidence of what a woman could do and would do if she took at notion. This much for preface, now for the story.

John A. Sylvester was a workman on the house and was left to finish up some inside work. While there, he asked Mrs. Lincoln if he could have a portion of the old cornice of the one-story building which had been removed to put on the second story. She told him to take all he wanted of it. He took two walnut boards one inch by eighteen inches wide and twelve feet long. John's father, Manuel Sylvester, was then an old man and a finished mechanic. He made a table of one of the boards and John made a cradle of the other. The cradle was used to rock John's babies in, and after it had served to rock Victor Sylvester, of Frank Simmons' art room, it was put in the stable loft and from thence was stolen. The table remained in the family until his family were all grown and was set aside. For some years, Mrs. Sylvester has been an invalid, requiring the constant

> care of her now aged husband, and to occupy his mind from brooding over his misfortune, John thought he would make something out of the old table as a memento of "Honest Old Abe." He has the box we referred to, which is finished elaborately and is a masterpiece of mechanism in every respect, containing, as we said before, 1,219 pieces inlaid. He has made another box, but it is much plainer and smaller. It is attracting a great deal of attention and will be exhibited at the World's fair, as it was packed and forwarded last night. The Monitor hopes that Mr. Sylvester may be able to realize something handsome out of his skill and industry. He has had his full share of misfortune and has grown quite thin in his devotion to his invalid wife.

One artifact—a prized collector's item—declares that Samuel S. Elder laid a tin roof on the Lincoln home in 1858, perhaps consummating the expansion for the rear wing of the Lincoln residence.[11] (The front wing was covered with a shingle roof.) Elder, a skilled tinsmith, was an ardent Republican[12] and later soldered the lead lining of Abraham Lincoln's casket after the final viewing of the body in Springfield on May 4, 1865.[13]

To identify John A. Sylvester, a brief history of this interesting family must be related. He was the son of Manuel (sometimes called Emanuel) Sylvester.[14] In 1853, a group of 273 immigrants came to Springfield, Illinois, from Madeira where the Roman Catholic Church had persecuted them beyond endurance. Among these Portuguese refugees were John A. Sylvester and his wife, Francisca J. Sylvester, who arrived in November that year, directly from New York where their ship had docked.[15] Sponsors for those immigrants were mostly members of the Presbyterian Church.

John A. Sylvester had been born at Madeira in 1827 and labored as a respected carpenter. His wife, likewise, had been born in Madeira on December 28, 1820.[16] Their first surviving child was named Mary Ellen and had been born in Madeira about 1850.[17] During their first years in Springfield, John and Francisca perhaps resided with the father of John. In a city directory for 1855-6, only "Emanuel" Sylvester is listed. A highly skilled carpenter, he lived at Washington, near Sixth Street.[18] It is certain, however, that John, his wife, and their first daughter came to the Capital City in 1853, because on March 31, 1856, the head of this household appeared in the Sangamon County circuit Court and filed his first papers for United States Citizenship. Then, on October 25, 1858, John once more presented himself, renounced his allegiance to Portugal and became an American citizen.[19] In those years, a person had to have resided in this country for five years before citizenship could be acquired. Thus, as he later stated, he came in 1853.

After assisting with the augmentation of the Lincoln dwelling, John A. Sylvester struck out on his own. He sheltered his growing family on Jefferson Street, between Twelfth and Thirteenth streets, a location later numbered 1219 East Jefferson.[20] Another daughter, named Sophia, was born in 1855. Then another girl, called Sarah, was born in 1857. Next, came John O., born in 1859. Following him, arrived Minnie, in 1862. And the last child, born in 1864, was Victor M. John O. graduated from high school in Springfield with the Class of 1879 and found employment with the Illinois Watch Factory in his home town. Victor M. worked as a picture framer for Frank Simmons.[21]

Mary Ellen Sylvester married John C. Roderick in Sangamon County on December 26, 1869. Sophia Sylvester married Henry H. Day in Morgan County on June 23, 1880. (He carried ice in Jacksonville.) Sarah Sylvester married John G. Vieira (also spelled Vierra) in Sangamon County on June 29, 1882. John O. Sylvester married Nellie Martin in Morgan County on June 11, 1884. (They later moved to Elgin, Illinois.) Minnie Sylvester married John F. Cherry, Jr., in Sangamon County on April 26, 1882. And Victor M. Sylvester married Etta M. Rogers in Sangamon County on November 30, 1887.[22]

Seven years older than her husband, Francisca J. Sylvester died at 9 p.m. on May 23, 1893, in her home, 1219 East Jefferson. She had been in ill health for several years; paralysis caused her demise. The Rev. Robert Reid Lennington,[23] on May 25, conducted funeral services at both the family residence and the First Portuguese Presbyterian Church where she had been a member.

Although not of Portuguese extraction, Rev. Lennington of Jacksonville served both the Jacksonville and the

Springfield Portuguese congregations. As a student, he had come to Jacksonville for training and later agreed to minister to these two churches. It was stated that Mrs. Sylvester had lived in Springfield ever since her arrival in 1853. The church was beautifully decorated with flowers, and its choir rendered several musical numbers. Following the last service, Francisca was buried in Oak Ridge Cemetery at Springfield.[24]

At 11:10 p.m. on November 12, 1895, John A. Sylvester passed away at his residence, 1219 East Jefferson. The Rev. Robert R. Lennington, still of Jacksonville, also conducted his funeral service in the home with burial in Oak Ridge Cemetery on the lot owned by his son-in-law, John G. Vieira. Thus passed from view another person who had known the immortal Abraham Lincoln and his family. Surviving him were four daughters: Mrs. John C. Roderick, Mrs. J.G. Vieira, Mrs. John F. Cherry and Mrs. Henry Day of Jacksonville. Two sons also remained: John O. Sylvester of Elgin, and Victor M. Sylvester of Springfield.[25]

Equally interesting and important to this Lincoln story is Abner Wilkinson, the man residing immediately across Eighth Street from the Lincolns. A city directory records his location in 1855—the very year in question—as on Eight at the corner of Jackson. His shop stood on Adams Street, near Fifth.[26] But his rented living quarters on Eighth were on Lot 9 of Block 7, a domicile generally identified as the William S. Burch property. The 1855 State Census also places him in the Lincoln neighborhood.[27] Wilkinson, who usually earned his living as a tailor, moved about continuously, according to the directories, and 1855 is probably the only year that he actually made his home opposite the Lincolns. This fact makes it all the more sure that the front building of the Lincoln's was raised in 1855, as stated in the interview with Sylvester.

Abner Wilkinson was born in Philadelphia, Pennsylvania, on July 16, 1817.[28] It is unknown at what time he removed to Springfield, Illinois, but he married Elizabeth Ann Brown in Sangamon County on June 17, 1847.[29] The bride was just sixteen. Often called Betsy or simply Ann, she was born about 1831 in Sangamon County, the daughter of Delos W. and Ruth (Morgan) Brown.[30] The Wilkinsons had at least six offspring: Robert D. born about 1849; Ada, born ca. 1852; Anna, born ca. 1855; Louis, born ca. 1857; John A., born in 1860; and Sallie, born ca. 1866.[31]

We first catch sight of Wilkinson as a businessman in 1848 when it was announced in the press that John Billington and Abner Wilkinson had on November 6 reopened Dickey's Bakery. They offered for sale bread, crackers, gingerbread, cakes, pies, ale and beer.[32] Another report stated that Billington had been raised to this trade,[33] but nothing is revealed about the experience of Wilkinson in this business.

John Dickey had arrived in Springfield about 1828. He died on June 3, 1846, at the age of sixty, being one of its oldest residents in length of time spent in Springfield.[34] Dickey had been an industrious entrepreneur operating out of his old stand on Washington Street, between Fourth and Fifth. In May of 1841, he even embarked upon a delivery service in which he ran a bread wagon that made its rounds to the homes of local inhabitants. He offered bread and cakes for sale from his wagon. It is not stated whether or not he would deliver beer, however.[35] When Mary Ann Todd suddenly proclaimed defiantly to her sister, Elizabeth (Todd) Edwards, at about noon on November 4, 1842, without any previous warning, that she and Abraham Lincoln were to be married that very evening, Elizabeth replied rather sarcastically: "Mary, you have not given me much time to prepare for our guests this evening." I guess," Elizabeth continued facetiously, "I will have to send to old Dickey's for some of his gingerbread and beer."[36] So John Dickey was a well-known fixture in the Springfield community and in this instance had a rather nebulous connection to the Lincoln legend, although he was not actually called upon to furnish "refreshments." Mrs. Edwards eventually gave in and baked the wedding cake herself.

Operating a bakery in Springfield in that era must have been a rather chancy undertaking when the proprietor or proprietors were not professional bakers with experience. Too, in that day, so many of the housewives did their own baking, even turning out loaves of bread. Very early, John Francis Rague, an architect from New York, opened a bakery about July 25, 1832. Yet, a newspaper editor titled Rague's advertisement as "Another Bakery."[37] Others who followed him were C.L.D. Crockwell, W.W. Watson, John Dulany, John W. Gray, Thomas Adams, etc.[38]

It would appear that Wilkinson was no baker, had no capital, or both. By December 18, 1849, John Billington had severed his connections with him, taken a new partner, Charles W. Graves, and moved their bakery to No. 5 Hoffman's Row, opposite the Post Office. There, the partners tried catering to the evening crowd as well as offering baked goods for sale during the day. From 8 to 9 p.m. they would even serve hot coffee, pies, etc.[39] Constructed in 1835, Hoffman's Row consisted of a connected set of six two-story brick buildings extending north from the corner of Fifth and Washington along the west side of Fifth. No sooner had Billington & Graves departed from old Dickey's location on Washington between Fourth and Fifth when Thomas Adams moved in and advertised "Fresh bread every day." He also made cakes, crackers, etc.[40] Fierce competition must have existed in this trade.

When the United States Census enumerator called at the Wilkinson residence on October 29, 1850, Abner had already become a tailor.[41] Early in the following year, William Harvey and Abner Wilkinson purchased the clothing establishment of Thomas S. Little on the south side of the Public Square. They, of course, did cutting and tailoring.[42] But—as with the bakery partnership—this arrangement was canceled on August 11, 1852, with Harvey remaining at the old location.[43]

With the advent of the 1850's, Wilkinson became more prominent in public affairs. On July 6, 1852, a program to honor the memory of Henry Clay started at the Protestant Episcopal Church, and from there a marching column continued on to the State Capitol upon the Public Square where the Hon. A. Lincoln gave the main eulogy in the Hall of the House. In addition to the Chief Marshal, there were four assistants: A. Wilkinson, C.W. Chatterton, D.J. Richardson and J.T. Smith.[44] Then on April 25, 1853, Wilkinson received an appointment to draft the by-laws for a new fire engine company. Presumably, he was also a member. He later was selected to solicit funds for this group, called The Friendship Fire Company No. 1.[45]

When his tailoring business seems to have dwindled in the next couple of years and city directories fail to list him at all, Wilkinson worked as a police officer. We know for sure that he testified at a trial in 1857 as the arresting officer.[46] Yet, by 1859, he is once more advertising as a tailor.[47] One thing we know for sure, in this period of his life, is that he was an ardent Democrat. This party's convention chose him to run for the office of Marshal of Springfield. However, at the April 3, 1860 election, he was soundly defeated.[48] And when the United States Census was taken in Springfield on August 6 of that year, Wilkinson once more gave his occupation as tailor.[49] But in the following years, he changed his partnerships and locations almost yearly.[50]

After a lingering illness, Elizabeth Ann (Brown) Wilkinson died on January 21, 1870, at the family residence on Walnut between Adams and Monroe. She was just thirty-nine years of age. Two days later, a funeral service was conducted at the Wilkinson home with burial at Oak Ridge Cemetery within the family burial plot purchased by Abner when an infant daughter, named Mary, died on August 21, 1865.[51]

A census enumerator questioned Abner Wilkinson on August 1, 1870, and learned that he considered himself a merchant now with $3000 worth of real estate and $3000 worth of personal estate.[52] With this amount of wealth, Abner determined to remarry. On October 7, 1872, he took to wife Margaret Ellen Soule—about 36 years of age. Born in about 1846, she came from Pennsylvania and had been residing prior to her marriage in the household of Frank Henry, the Springfield City Clerk, also born in Pennsylvania.[53] Miss Soule's father was a native of France, but her mother came from Ireland.[54]

Even after Abraham Lincoln died in 1865, Abner Wilkinson had at least one more connection with the Lincoln saga. In 1876, Wilkinson was Springfield's Chief of Police. While making his official rounds of the town in June, he changed to speak with the operator of a brothel. That man informed Wilkinson that a drunken patron had boasted about his connection with a plot to "steal old

Lincoln's bones." Wilkinson quickly informed the Custodian of the Lincoln Tomb about his nefarious scheme, and precautions were taken for the revealed crime date of July 4 that year. But since the conspiracy had become noised about town, the abduction plan was called off by the perpetrators. Nevertheless, another unsuccessful attempted theft of Lincoln's body did take place on November 7 that same year.[55]

Sometime in 1882, the Wilkinsons left Springfield and moved to LaCrosse, Wisconsin, where Abner found employment as a cutter and tailor for George Scharpf. After twenty-one years in that city, Abner succumbed at his residence, 813 Jackson Street, at 4:30 p.m. on July 1, 1903. Cerebral hyperemia, coupled with chronic rheumatism, caused his demise. He had suffered with severe pain for many years. Dying at the age of eighty-six, he left a wife (Margaret Ellen), three daughters and two sons.

After a funeral service at the family home by the Rev. C.N. Moller on July 3, the body was shipped to Springfield, Illinois, for burial beside his first wife in Oak Ridge Cemetery. T.C. Smith, a local funeral director, met the train and took charge of the casket and all necessary arrangements. On the following day, the Venerable Frederick A. DeRosset, M.A., Rector of St. Paul's Pro-Cathedral Church, delivered the final obsequies. Thus ended the earthly history of a man who had lived across from the Lincolns on Eight Street in 1855.[56] Having been an ardent Democrat, however, Wilkinson certainly never supported Abraham Lincoln's political endeavors and seems to have left no reminiscences of him.

We cannot close this volume without mentioning some interesting visitors to the Lincoln Home. Neither of them stayed there, but both of them did some writing while in the home. One was Dale Carnegie, who wrote in his book, *Lincoln the Unknown:* "Many of the chapters were written in Springfield. Some in the sitting-room of the old home where Lincoln lived for sixteen unhappy years. . . ."[57] Another writer who worked at the Lincoln Home was the publisher of this book, Doris Replogle Wenzel (formerly Doris Replogle Porter) who wrote a play in the summer of 1981, *Without Discretion*, based on the life of Mary (Todd) Lincoln. During her research in Springfield, Wenzel wrote most of the "Springfield" scenes of the play while sitting on the South porch of the Lincoln Home.[58]

On June 17, 1990, the famous artist, Dr. Lloyd Ostendorf, set up his easel in the front bedroom of the Lincoln Home and drew Abraham Lincoln as a young man and then proceeded to age him while Ed Janik recorded this unique event with a movie camera. Participating in this historic event were the author, his wife, Sunderine, Rita Ostendorf and Phil Wagner.

References

1 Mrs. John Todd Stuart to Bettie Stuart, Springfield, Ill., Apr. 3, 1856, MS., John T. Stuart-Milton Hay Coll., Illinois State Historical Library; *Daily Illinois State Journal* (Springfield), Jan. 6, 1857, p. 2, c. 6.

2 Roy P. Basler, Marion D. Pratt and Lloyd A. Dunlap, eds., *The Collected Works of Abraham Lincoln* (New Brunswick: Rutgers Univ. Press, 1953), II, 79-80.

3 Earl Schenck Miers, ed., *Lincoln Day by Day* (Washington: Lincoln Sesquicentennial Commission, 1960), II, 146; Basler, ed., *The Collected Works*, II, 343-344.

4 Katherine Helm, *The True Story of Mary, Wife of Lincoln* (N.Y.: Harper & Bros., 1928), 106-107.

5 Luann Elvey to Wayne C. Temple, Chicago, Ill., Dec. 18, 1985.

6 Jane Maria Barrett, daughter of James and Mariah Barrett, was born in Island Grove Twp. of Sangamon Co., Ill., on May 31, 1836. She married Charles Ridgely, a member of a most prominent Springfield family, on June 10, 1857. She died in Eustis, Fla., on Mar. 15, 1922, and was buried in Oak Ridge Cemetery at Springfield. U.S. Census 1850, Island Grove Twp., Sangamon Co., Ill, p. 221 B, 11. 3-7; Marriage License, Sangamon Co.; *Illinois State Journal*, Mar. 16, 1922, p. 1, cc. 3-5.

7 The World's Columbian Exposition was held in Chicago from May 1 to Oct. 30, 1893.

8 Hannon & Ragsdale hired Charles Dallman and Alexander Graham as carpenters on this expansion project. *Illinois State Register* (Springfield), Feb. 27, 1938, p. 2, cc. 2-4.

9 On the spring circuit, Lincoln traveled from April 2 until June 4, 1855, but he returned to Springfield several times during this period.

Miers, ed., *Lincoln Day by Day*, II, 141-146.

10 James Gourley, a shoemaker from Pennsylvania once living between 1850 and 1857 on Lot 9 of Block 10 almost directly behind the Lincoln residence, also related this tale, but Abner Wilkinson would have been in a better location to hear Mr. Lincoln make these humorous remarks in person since the latter resided immediately across Eighth Street from the Lincolns. Lawyer Lincoln, no doubt, came down this street to enter his front door. In the middle 1850's, Lincoln would have been traveling by train and not by horse and buggy which would have necessitated driving to his barn at the rear of his home where Gourley might have encountered him. Emanuel Hertz, ed., *The Hidden Lincoln* (N.Y.: The Viking Press, 1938), 383. Wilkinson, without doubt, passed this anecdote around to his neighbors who then repeated it to others until it became rather common knowledge in Springfield. The story of the man who left a wife and baby for a trip to California also sounds like a typical Lincoln canard.

11 This artifact has written upon it: "Tin plate from roof of Lincoln Home, Springfield, Ill. Roof installed 1858 by S.S. Elder. Tin removed 1901 by J.C. Neuman. Tray by J.C. Neuman." This original pin tray owned now by Jean Fisherkeller, Springfield, Ill.

12 *Illinois State Journal*, Apr. 10, 1875, p. 4, c. 6.

13 Wayne C. Temple, "Tinsmith to the Late Mr. Lincoln: Samuel S. Elder," *Jour. Ill. State Hist. Soc.*, LXXI, 176-184 (Aug., 1978).

14 *Sangamo Monitor*, Apr. 5, 1893, clipping.

15 *Illinois State Journal*, May 24, 1893, p. 5, c. 5.

16 U.S. Census 1860, Springfield, Sangamon Co., Ill., p. 112, ll. 30-35; *Illinois State Journal*, May 24, 1893, p. 5, c. 5.

17 U.S. Census 1860, Springfield, Sangamon Co., Ill., p. 112, l. 32

18 *Springfield City Directory. . . For 1855-6* (Springfield: Birchall & Owen, 1855), 39.

19 Record of Naturalization, Sangamon Co., Ill., I, 59, Microfilm, Illinois State Archives.

20 *Buck & Kriegh's City Directory For the Year 1859* (Springfield: B.A. Richards & Co., 1859), 73.

21 U.S. Census 1860, Springfield, Sangamon Co., Ill. , p. 112, 11. 30-35; U.S. Census 1870, Springfield, Sangamon Co., Ill., p. 36, 11. 15-21; U.S. Census 1880, Springfield, Sangamon, Co., Ill., E.D. 220, p. 6, 11. 42-48; *History of Sangamon County, Illinois* (Chicago: Inter-State Pub. Co., 1881), 596.

22 Illinois Marriage Records on computer at the Illinois State Archives.

23 Session minutes of the Portuguese Presbyterian Church at Springfield spelled his name as "Lenington." However, city directories and other records give it as "Lennington."

24 *Daily Illinois State Journal*, May 24, 1893, p. 5, c. 5, May 25, 1893, p. 5, c. 5, May 26, 1893, p. 4, c. 4. Her son-in-law, John G. Vieira, purchased a burial plot in Oak Ridge Cemetery on May 24, 1893, just the day after Francisca died, and her husband was later buried there in 1895, but cemetery records for this purchase (Block 11, Lot 9 W 1/2) do not show Francisca buried there. Nevertheless, she most certainly is interred in this lot. There are no markers on the graves. Oak Ridge Cemetery Records, Springfield.

25 *Daily Illinois State Journal*, Nov. 13, 1895, p. 5, c. 5, Nov. 14, 1895, p. 5, c. 5 and Oak Ridge Cemetery Records. The First Portuguese Presbyterian Church at this time was at Seventh and Reynolds. *Springfield City Directory* (Springfield: Springfield Directory Co., 1894), 22. Also buried on the family cemetery lot in Springfield are:

Henry H. Day (Aug. 5, 1851-Nov. 10, 1934) who died in Jacksonville, Morgan Co., Ill., and his wife, Sophia (Sylvester) Day (Mar. 17, 1855-Oct. 29, 1935) who died in Springfield. Death Records Nos. 44964 and 40941, Ill. Dept. of Public Health: Vital Records, Springfield.

26 *Springfield City Director. . .For 1855-6* (Springfield: Birchall & Owen, 1855), 43, 46. This directory was compiled and published in 1855.

27 Illinois State Census 1855, Springfield, Sangamon Co., p. 125, 1. 2.

28 Wisconsin Death Records, LaCross Co., II, 145, MS., Madison, Wis.

29 Sangamon County Marriage Licenses, II, 265, MS., Sangamon Co. Bldg.

30 *Illinois State Register*, Jan. 22, 1870, p. 1, c. 5; Delos W. Brown was born in Hartford, Conn., on Oct. 28, 1803, and married Ruth Morgan in Sangamon Co., Ill., on February 25, 1825. This couple had three children of whom one was Elizabeth Ann. John Carroll Power, *History of the Early Settlers of Sangamon County, Illinois* (Springfield: Edwin A. Wilson & Co., 1876), 152; Sangamon Co. Marriage Licenses.

31 U.S. Census 1850, Springfield, Sangamon Co., Ill., p. 108B, 11. 16-19; *ibid*., 1860, p. 557, 11. 21-26; *ibid*., 1870, p. 477, 11. 18-24.

32 *Illinois State Journal*, Nov. 8, 1848, p. 3, c. 5.

33 *Ibid*., Aug. 22, 1849, p. 1, c. 6.

34 *Sangamo Journal*, June 4, 1846, p. 3, c. 1.

35 *Ibid*., May 14, 1841, p. 3, c. 7.

36 Reminiscences of Mrs. Benjamin Stephenson Edwards, MS., Lincoln Public Library, Springfield, Ill. B.S. Edwards was a brother of

Ninian Wirt Edwards who was married to Elizabeth Todd, sister of Mary Ann Todd.

37 *Sangamo Journal*, July 26, 1832, p. 3 c. 3.

38 *Ibid*., Aug. 23, 1834, p. 3, c. 6, Sept. 17, 1836, p. 2, c. 7, June 7, 1839, p. 3, c. 1, Nov. 1, 1839, p. 4, c. 4, May 14, 1841, p. 3, c. 4, Aug. 22, 1849, p. 2, c. 1.

39 *Illinois Daily Journal*, Dec. 19, 1849, p. 3, c. 1.

40 *Ibid*., Jan. 24, 1850, p. 3, c. 1.

41 U.S. Census 1850, Springfield, Sangamon Co., Ill., p. 108B, 11. 16-19.

42 *Illinois Daily Journal*, Feb. 8, 1851, p. 3. c. 1.

43 *Ibid*., Aug. 11, 1852, p. 3, c. 2.

44 *Ibid*., July 6, 1852, p. 2, c. 1.

45 *Ibid*., Apr. 27, 1853, p. 3, c. 1; May 12, 1853, p. 3, c. 2.

46 *Ibid*., May 2, 1857, p. 2, c. 4. It is common practice not to list the residence of a police officer.

47 *Buck & Kriegh's City Directory for 1859* (Springfield: B.A. Richards & Co., 1859), 78.

48 *Illinois State Journal*, Mar. 20, 1860, p. 3, cc. 2-3, Apr. 4, 1860, p. 3, c. 2.

49 U.S. Census 1860, Springfield, Sangamon Co., Ill., p. 557, 11. 21-26.

50 Springfield city directories for these years.

51 *Illinois State Register*, Jan. 22, 1870, p. 1, c. 5; Oak Ridge Cemetery Records. Their plot was Lot 63 in Block 12. Also buried here are a son, Louis Wilkinson, died Dec. 7, 1896, and another son, John A. Wilkinson, died Oct. 5, 1920, as a result of suicide. The latter was single.

52 U.S. Census 1870, Springfield, Sangamon Co., Ill., p. 477, 11. 18-24.

53 *Ibid.*, p. 273, 11. 34-39; Sangamon Co. Marriage Licenses, IV, 528.

54 U.S. Census 1880, Springfield, Sangamon Co., Ill., E.D. 223, p. 14, 11. 38-41.

55 John Carroll Power, *History of an Attempt to Steal the Body of Abraham Lincoln* (Springfield: H.W. Rokker Printing, 1890), 14-17. When Abner's son, Louis Wilkinson, died at 4th and Washington on Dec. 7, 1896, his obituary identified him as the son of Captain Wilkinson, formerly Marshal of Springfield. *Illinois State Journal*, Dec. 8, 1896, p. 6, c. 4.

56 Wisconsin Death Records, LaCross County, II, 145; *The LaCross Leader Press*, July 2, 1903, p. 8; *Illinois State Journal*, July 4, 1903, p. 6, c. 3; *Polk's Springfield City Directory 1902-1903* (Springfield: R.L. Polk & Co., 1902), 25, 177; Oak Ridge Cemetery Records. Cerebral hyperemia would be an excess of blood in the brain, indicating a bursting of a blood vessel there.

57 Dale Carnegie, *Lincoln the Unknown* (Garden City, N.Y.: Dale Carnegie & Assoc., 1932), ix-x.

58 Doris (Replogle) Porter (now Wenzel), *Without Discretion*, a 3-act play based on the life of Mary (Todd) Lincoln. Research funded by the Richter Fellowship and produced by North Central College, Nov. 1981. A 2-act version of the play was produced at the Chicago Playwrights Center, 1984. Author received Lincoln Academy Award for play, Fall, 1981.

OFFICE OF THE SECRETARY OF STATE
SPRINGFIELD

CHARLES F. CARPENTIER
SECRETARY OF STATE

This picture of Abraham Lincoln is the one he used during his campaign for the presidency of the United States in 1860. It was taken on a Sunday, June 3, 1860, in the State Capitol building, the structure which is now the Sangamon County courthouse, by Alexander Hesler, a Chicago photographer.

In those days, photographers used wet, glass plates, and it was common practice for them to reclaim the glass by dipping it in an acid bath to remove the collodion which carried the picture. Somehow, the Lincoln picture escaped that fate.

In 1866, about a year after Lincoln was assassinated, Hesler's studio passed into the hands of George B. Ayres. The full impact of the Emancipator's greatness had not yet dawned on the people, but Ayres decided to keep the negatives as mementos. A year later he sold the studio and moved to the East, taking the negatives with him. Five weeks later the studio was burned out.

Ayres left the negatives to two daughters, and in 1932, a Philadelphia attorney accepted them in lieu of a fee and a debt of $500 on the estate of one of the daughters. When the attorney attempted to send them by mail to St. Louis, the negatives were broken, making it impossible to obtain any further prints from them. They were turned over to the Smithsonian Institute.

These were believed to be the only extant negatives of the historic picture until the fall of 1952, when King V. Hostick, Springfield collector of historical documents, found a duplicate set of negatives in an assortment of effects he bought in Philadelphia from the estate of Ayres. This print was made from one of those negatives.

Sincerely yours,

Charles F. Carpentier

Secretary of State

Copy of Carpentier's Letter regarding the Lincoln photo on page 4.

Additional Material

Occupants of Home

1839-1844	Rev. Charles Dresser
1844-1847	Lincoln
1847-1848	Cornelius Ludlum
1848-1849	Mason Brayman
1849-1861	Lincoln
1861-1869	Lucian Tilton
1869-1877	George Harlow
1877-1878	Jacob D. Akard
1878-1879	Vacant
1879-1883	Dr. Gustav Wendlandt
1883-1893	Osborn H. Oldroyd

Custodians for the State of Illinois

1893-1897	Herman Hofferkamp
1887-1893	Osborn H. Oldroyd
1893-1897	Herman Hofferkamp
1897-1915	Albert S. Edwards
1915-1918	Josephine Edwards
1918-1924	Mary (Edwards) Brown
1924-1953	Virginia (Stuart) Brown
1953-1958	Kathleen S. Bradish (she did not live in the Home)
1958-1972`	Kept open by Guides employed by IL Dept. of Conservation, Parks & Memorials Division

Superintendents for U.S.

1972-1982	Albert W. Banton
1982-1987	James T. O'Toole

1987-1990	Gentry Davis
1990-	Norman D. Hellmers

Chronology of Ownership

1836	Surveyed and platted for Elijah Iles who sold Lot 8 to Dr. Gershom Jayne
1839	Original Lot bought by Charles Dresser from Dr. Jayne
1839	Additional 10 feet purchased by Dresser from Francis Webster, Jr.
1839	Original home built by John & Page Eaton for Rev. Dresser
1844	Sold to A. Lincoln
1855-56	Second story added by Lincoln
1887	Conveyed by Robert T. Lincoln to State of Illinois
1972	Title transferred from State of Illinois to the Federal Government

The following index was originally designed for the first edition of this book, *By Square and Compasses: The Building of Lincoln's Home and Its Saga*, now out of print, by Louis L. Williams and revised for this edition.

Index

Also see References

—A—

—C—

—G—

—H—

—J—

—K—

—L—

—M—

—Mc—

—N—

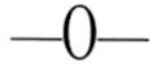

—O—

—P—

—R—

—T—

—U—

—V—

—W—

—XYZ—

Other Books of History by Mayhaven Publishing

Abraham Lincoln: From Skeptic to Prophet
Wayne C. Temple

America's Rural Hub
Stanley A. Changnon

An Unofficial History of Mahomet, Illinois
Isabelle S. Purnell

Basil Moore's Lincoln
Basil W. Moore

Beijing Odyssey: Based on the Life & Times of Liang Shiyi
Steven T. Au

Broomcorn Johnnies
Richard L. Thomas

Chicken Tommy & Other Stories
Richard L. Thomas

Dear Family
Marjorie Heaton Lynn

Our Church: 100th Anniversary of Osman Lutheran Church
The 100th Anniversary Committee

The Many Faces of Lincoln
Selected Articles from The Lincoln Herald
Edited by Charles M. Hubbard, Thomas R. Turner and Steven K. Rogstad

Note: Dr. Temple is a prolific writer and has authored many volumes with a variety of publishers